Diagnosis and Treatment of Dissociative Disorders

Diagnosis and Treatment of Dissociative Disorders

Edited by
Jon G. Allen, Ph.D. &
William H. Smith, Ph.D.

JASON ARONSON INC.
Northvale, New Jersey
London

The original source of this material is *The Bulletin of the Menninger Clinic,* Summer 1993, vol. 57 (3) 285-399. Copyright © 1993 The Menninger Foundation. This book was printed and bound by Haddon Craftsmen of Scranton, Pennsylvania.

10 9 8 7 6 5 4 3 2 1

Library of Congress Cataloging-in-Publication Data

Diagnosis and treatment of dissociative disorders / edited by Jon G.
Allen and William H. Smith.
    p.   cm.
    "Original source of this material is *The Bulletin of the Menninger
Clinic,* summer 1993, vol. 57 (3) 285-399"—T.p. verso.
    Includes bibliographical references.
    ISBN 1-56821-275-5
    1. Dissociative disorders. I. Allen, Jon G. II. Smith, William
H. (William Hugh), 1940-   . III. Bulletin of the Menninger Clinic.
    [DNLM: 1. Dissociative Disorders—diagnosis. 2. Dissociative
Disorders—therapy.   WM 173.6 D536   1995]
RC553.D5D52   1994
616.85′23 — dc20
DNLM/DLC
for Library of Congress   94-27324

Manufactured in the United States of America. Jason Aronson Inc. offers books and cassettes. For information and catalog write to Jason Aronson Inc., 230 Livingston Street, Northvale, New Jersey 07647.

Contents

Introduction

Jon G. Allen, PhD

The seeming epidemic of patients with dissociative symptoms related to a history of trauma has generated an intellectual scramble in the mental health field. Many astute thinkers and clinicians have labored during the past decade to develop specialized expertise in the diagnosis and treatment of patients who have experienced trauma and subsequent dissociative disorders. Now this hard-won knowledge needs to be widely assimilated and disseminated. Centers and clinics for the treatment of sequelae of sexual abuse have sprung up throughout the country. Expertise cannot be confined to a limited cadre of specialists; there is a widespread need and demand for clinical understanding and effective treatment.

At The Menninger Clinic as elsewhere, we have seen a dramatic increase in recent years in the incidence of dissociative disorders. We convened a task force on sexual abuse and dissociative disorders and subsequently created an inpatient unit to specialize in the treatment of patients with trauma-related disorders. The inpatient unit focuses on two prevalent symptom patterns—dissociation and self-harm. This unit is a key component of the Trauma Recovery Program, which provides a continuum of services, including inpatient, partial hospital, and outpatient treatment.

For the past several years, the social work discipline of The Menninger Clinic has sponsored an annual continuing education conference. In 1992, for the first time, the conference was devoted to dissociative disorders, and it provided a nucleus of papers first published in the *Bulletin of the Menninger Clinic* and now presented in this book. The conference presenters, like the authors of these papers, were primarily Menninger staff members involved in the task force and the Trauma Recovery Program. Presenters were encouraged to develop their papers for publication, and the papers were peer-reviewed for inclusion here.

The first four papers in this book lay some groundwork: My paper on the working model of dissociative processes provides a broad theoretical base for a method to educate patients about dissociation. We have also included a paper by Bruce Reis from the Trauma Clinic at Massachusetts General Hospital; Dr. Reis's paper examines dissociation from a psychoanalytic perspective. The next paper, by Kathryn Zerbe, offers a psychodynamic understanding of the link between eating disorders and dissociative disorders. The following paper, by William Smith and me,

---

Dr. Allen is a senior staff psychologist in the Trauma Recovery Program at The Menninger Clinic.

summarizes current methods employed in the diagnosis of dissociative disorders.

The six papers concluding this book illustrate the efforts of Menninger clinicians from various professional disciplines in several clinical contexts to translate specialized knowledge into effective treatment. The first two papers focus on interventions specific to dissociative disorders in individual psychotherapy. William Smith articulates the relationship between hypnosis and dissociation and delineates the various uses of hypnosis in the treatment of MPD. Carolyn Grame addresses the importance of helping patients to contain traumatic affect and describes some of the methods she employs in the psychotherapy process. Bonnie Buchele conveys the challenge that patients with dissociative disorders pose for group psychotherapy and describes ways of working with such patients to enable them to make use of this powerful modality. Sue Porter, Kay Kelly, and Carolyn Grame present the approaches they have evolved in family work with children and spouses of patients with MPD. Catherine Pawlicki and Carol Gaumer focus on a major challenge in inpatient nursing care: managing self-mutilation in patients with dissociative disorders. Finally, Kay Kelly describes methods that have been developed to work with MPD patients in a partial hospital setting.

The treatment of dissociative disorders is rife with controversy, and we harbor no illusions of presenting the final word. The following is our progress report.

1. Dissociative Processes: Theoretical Underpinnings of a Working Model for Clinician and Patient

Jon G. Allen, PhD

Dissociative symptoms are now widely recognized, but they are nevertheless challenging for clinicians and bewildering to patients. The author presents a conceptual framework for understanding dissociative processes, emphasizing discontinuity in experience and delineating various junctures in the unfolding of dissociative episodes. The conceptual framework provides the theoretical underpinnings for a simple schema that can be used to explain dissociation to patients and to help them articulate their dissociative experience.

How would you explain dissociation to a patient? Dissociation is devilishly complicated, largely because it is tangled up with our perennial nemesis, consciousness. Simplifying such a complex phenomenon for didactic purposes is a peculiarly ambitious task. Working backward from complexity to simplicity, I will review diverse literature to provide some conceptual moorings for a schematic model of dissociative processes. This simple schema has proved useful in educating patients about dissociation and providing them with a handy framework to articulate their individual experience.

This paper takes a somewhat circuitous route to the simple teaching device by beginning with some theoretical underpinnings. To put contemporary concepts of dissociation in context, we must take note of Janet's contributions. After this nod to history, current concepts of dissociation will be reviewed, with particular emphasis on the discontinuity in experience engendered by dissociation. As will become evident, discontinuity and continuity are two sides of the coin of consciousness; each must be understood in relation to the other. Accordingly, the introductory excursion will include discussion of the key contributors to the continuity of experience.

This article is based on a presentation at a Menninger Continuing Education conference, "Dissociative States: Multiple Personality and Other Trauma-Related Disorders," held February 14-16, 1992, at Topeka, Kansas. Dr. Allen is a senior staff psychologist in the Trauma Recovery Program at The Menninger Clinic. The author is grateful to Richard Kluft, MD, for his careful review and perceptive critique of the manuscript and for his guidance throughout the process of revision; to Frank Putnam, MD, and David Spiegel, MD, for serving as referees without the benefit of anonymity; and to Bonnie Buchele, PhD, James Eyman, PhD, Glen Gabbard, MD, and William Smith, PhD, for their helpful comments and suggestions.

1

A historical note

Preoccupation with trauma and dissociation is both new and old. In struggling to reconcile trauma theory and psychodynamic thinking, we are resurrecting the century-old clash between Freud and Janet (Ellenberger, 1970; Gabbard, 1994; Loewenstein & Ross, 1992; Perry & Laurence, 1984; van der Hart & Friedman, 1989). Although these two pioneers began on parallel tracks, viewing traumatic experience as paramount in the etiology of symptoms, Freud turned his gaze inward to intrapsychic conflict, whereas Janet continued to evolve a trauma theory. Using Kuhn's (1962) terminology for scientific revolutions, the current focus on trauma has been construed as a paradigm shift (Loewenstein & Ross, 1992). This apparent sea change, however, can also be seen more modestly as an attempt to pick up where Janet left off. Indeed, it is humbling to discover that Janet's clinical descriptions, theoretical accounts, and treatment approaches are utterly contemporary. Certainly his clinical experience was no less dramatic than ours. Witness the following example of reenactment of trauma:

A man of thirty-two ... usually remains in bed, for both his legs are paralyzed.... In the middle of the night he rises slowly, jumps lightly out of bed, for the paralysis we have just spoken of has quite vanished, takes his pillow and hugs it. We know by his countenance and by his words that he mistakes this pillow for his child, and that he believes he is saving his child from the hands of his mother-in-law. Then, bearing that weight, he tries to slip out of the room, opens the door, and runs out through the court-yard; climbing along the gutter, he gets to the housetop, carrying his pillow and running all about the buildings of the hospital with marvelous agility. One must take great care to catch him, and use all sorts of cautions to get him down, for he wakes with a stupefied air, and as soon as he is awake, both his legs are paralyzed again, and he must be carried to his bed. He does not understand what you are speaking about, and cannot comprehend how it happens that people were obliged to go to the top of the house in order to look for a poor man who has been paralyzed in his bed for months. (Janet, 1907, pp. 28-29)

Defining dissociation

Such dramatic dissociative episodes have again become common clinical fare. Janet's description illustrates well the *DSM-III-R* (American Psychiatric Association, 1987) definition of dissociation as "a disturbance or alteration in the normally integrative functions of identity, memory, or consciousness" (p. 269). Spiegel and Cardeña (1991) characterized dissociation as "a structured separation of mental processes (e.g., thoughts, emotions, conation, memory, and identity) that are ordinarily integrated" (p. 367). Furthermore, these separated mental processes tend to be mutually exclusive: "Dissociation as a model of defense ... carries with it the implication of two or more incompatible mental contents that are structured so as to exclude one another from consciousness" (Spiegel, 1990, p. 126). The dissociating patient is separating and excluding mental processes and contents that are normally integrated. She or he is unable to think about two or more contents in connection with one another, perhaps instead alternating among contradictory experiences.

Just what is separated or excluded from what? A short answer: To a degree, the self is separated from its own experience. Aspects of the self are segregated, and realms of experience are relegated to a "not-me" domain. Kihlstrom (1984; Kihlstrom & Hoyt, 1990) emphasized that dissociation works on episodic memory (memory for experienced events) and, more specifically, autobiographical memory. In effect, dissociation can delete the organismic, spatiotemporal context normally associated with memory for events. Dissociated mental contents—images, ideas, affects—are active and they impinge on consciousness, but they are not consciously linked with one's own history or sense of self. Kihlstrom and Hoyt (1990) usefully distinguished among conscious, preconscious, and subconscious processes, the latter being central to dissociation:

The essential distinction between what is conscious and what is not is that conscious mental contents are both activated (by perception or thought) and linked with activated representations of the self, its goals, and its local environment. Preconscious mental contents are latent: not activated (or, more properly, not activated above some threshold) and perforce not linked to the activated mental representation of the self. Dissociated, subconscious mental contents, while fully activated, are not linked with either an active mental representation of the self or the active mental representation of the context, or both. (p. 201)

Why separate oneself from aspects of one's experience? Many traumatized individuals learned to separate themselves from their experience because the experience was unbearable. Emphasizing its defensive aspects, Young (1988) defined dissociation as "an active inhibitory process that normally screens internal and external stimuli from the field of consciousness," viewing it as a "shut-off mechanism to prevent over-stimulation or flooding of consciousness by excessive incoming stimuli" (p. 35). He noted that dissociation can serve the normal role of enhancing "the integrating functions of the ego by screening out excessive or irrelevant stimuli" but that, under pathological conditions, dissociation is employed defensively, resulting in "an interruption of integrating functions" (p. 36).

Dissociation is not invariably linked to trauma (Spiegel & Cardeña, 1991), and this form of self-protection is not available to all persons. Dissociation is properly considered a skill, and the capacity for dissociation certainly plays a prominent role in hypnotic talent. This skill can be viewed as an ability to manipulate attention in various ways (Kihlstrom & Hoyt, 1990). Moreover, dissociation covers a broad spectrum of experience (Braun, 1988a; Putnam, 1991a), ranging from transient episodes of "spacing out" to multiple personality disorder (MPD). Thus patients may find it helpful to think of themselves as using a "skill" in a wide range of contexts. But they developed it in dire circumstances. The skill becomes a crippling defense. Not everyone is constitutionally equipped to use the defense of dissociation; not everyone who is traumatized develops a dissociative disorder. A predisposition to dissociate is a necessary etiological condition (Braun, 1988b; Braun & Sachs, 1985; Kluft, 1984).

How does dissociation relate to other defenses? Gabbard (1994) reviewed current literature on this complex problem, carefully teasing apart the relationships between dissociation and other defenses. He pointed out that, whereas repression maintains material in the dynamic unconscious, dissociation maintains material in a series of parallel consciousnesses. In addition, repression defends against forbidden internal wishes, whereas dissociation defends against traumatic experiences associated with external events. Gabbard also systematically compared and contrasted dissociation and splitting, viewing dissociation as broader than splitting (creating a wider variety of divisions) and emphasizing the specific impact of dissociation on memory and consciousness. Yet he noted that dissociation not only divides the self; like splitting, it divides patterns of object relationships.

The ordinary continuity of experience

To reiterate: In the service of protecting the self from unbearable experience, those who have the mental agility to do so are able to segregate various aspects of their experience. To understand fully the operation of this defense, it is essential to appreciate its counterpart, the continuity of experience. We are inclined to take it for granted, but Spiegel (1991) pointed out that "the continuity of experience, memory, and identity is an accomplishment" (p. 143). This continuity depends on the reciprocal of dissociation, *association*; it is a continual construction. Ordinarily, we keep a running record of experience available to conscious access. Popper (1977) referred to "continuity-producing memory," which "draws, unconsciously, a spatio-temporal track of our immediate past, like the trail of an aeroplane in the sky, or like the track of a skier in the snow; a track that with the passing of time becomes somewhat indistinct" (p. 131).

Understanding the basis of continuity of experience is a major challenge and far beyond the scope of this paper. For present purposes, three key constituents can be highlighted: self-organization, memory/affect, and consciousness.

Self-organization

In much contemporary theory, the self has been accorded the top job of running the mind. The self belongs at the top of the hierarchy insofar as it comprises ultimate goals, values, and convictions. Kohut (1979) defined the self as "a unit, cohesive in space and enduring in time, which is a center of initiative and a recipient of impressions" (p. 452). The self as active agent can be distinguished from the self-concept, that is, the self's ideas about itself (i.e., the self is the "I" and the self-concept is the "me"). If the self is construed as the ultimate organizer of experience, tied to overarching goals, maintaining self-organization and integration is ordinarily the highest priority of the mind. As Spiegel (1988) argued, it is the "loss of control over one's own state of mind that constitutes the full depth of post-traumatic symptomatology" (p. 19).

It is also important to recognize that, although the self is intrapsychic, it is largely created through interpersonal relationships. That is, an overriding set of goals has to do with creating and maintaining relationships. As Popper (1977) maintained, the self "owes this selfhood largely to interaction with other persons, other selves, and with ... [culture]" (p. 120). Horowitz (1991a) has articulated psychological structure in terms of person schemas, role relationship models, and complex configurations of relationships. Organizing this psychological architecture are "self schemas" at various hierarchical levels; Horowitz defined self-organization as "the overall referent to a person's set of available schemas and supraordinate schemas" (p. 7).

Memory/affect

To maintain continuity of experience, the self is fundamentally dependent on memory:

Memory collects the countless phenomena of our existence into a single whole; and, as our bodies would be scattered into the dust of

5

*their component atoms if they were not held together by the attrac-
tion of matter, so our consciousness would be broken up into as many
fragments as we had lived seconds but for the binding and unifying
force of memory. (Hering, quoted in Schacter, 1989, p. 683)*

Just as there would be no continuity without memory, there would be
no posttraumatic stress disorder and no dissociation without memory.
Memory is multifaceted (see Schacter, 1989), and Kihlstrom (1984,
1987) has provided a taxonomy pertinent to dissociative disorders. Most
generally, procedural (implicit) and declarative (explicit) memory must
be distinguished. Procedural memory (e.g., motor skills, grammatical
structure) is inherently unconscious. Declarative memory comprises all
episodic memory and much semantic memory: "Episodic memory is
autobiographical memory, concerning one's own past experiences and
referring to the spatiotemporal and organismic context in which those
experiences occurred; semantic memory may be thought of as the mental
lexicon of categorical world knowledge stored without reference to the
episodic context in which it has been acquired and used" (Kihlstrom
& Hoyt, 1990, p. 196). Declarative memory may be conscious,
preconscious (readily accessible to consciousness), or subconscious
(dissociated, that is, lacking autobiographical context).

The continuity of self-experience is inextricably linked to autobiographical memory. Brewer (1986) counseled against equating autobiographical with episodic memory. He defined autobiographical memory
as "memory for information related to the self" (p. 26) and proposed
that autobiographical memory itself is multifaceted. He distinguished
among personal memories (unique events such as one's high school
graduation), generic personal memories (repeated experiences such as
trips to grandmother's house), and autobiographical facts (knowledge
about one's life experience). Personal memories are heavily laden with
imagery, especially visual imagery. Brewer noted that "a personal
memory is accompanied by a belief that the remembered episode was
personally experienced by the self" (p. 34) and "by a belief that it
occurred in the self's past" (pp. 34-35).

Memory contributes to the continuity of experience by providing
the basis for interpreting ongoing perception. One's history and current
experience are continuously interwoven. Importantly, this process is
predominantly unconscious. Kihlstrom (1984) summarized:

*Incoming stimuli are first processed by the sensory-perceptual
system. The operation of this system is unconscious, in the sense
that it is involuntary and the perceiver has no direct introspective
access to it. Similarly, the stored procedural knowledge which guides*

this perceptual processing is unconscious.... [The] conscious percept is the product of the interaction between data driven ("bottom-up") and conceptually driven ("top-down") cognitive activity. Not all of the declarative knowledge available in memory is activated and thus represented in consciousness; but what is accessed and brought into consciousness is determined by contributions from both the perceiver and the perceptual world. (pp. 168-169)

Edelman (1989, 1992) pointed out that perceptions are interpreted specifically in relation to "value-category memory," namely, the set of memories associated with intrinsic biological values (hedonic and homeostatic set points established by natural selection). Consciousness emerges in the momentary synthesis of current perceptual novelty with prior value-category memory; consciousness is the "remembered present." Extending Edelman's work to the context of trauma, one would think that traumatic autobiographical memories would comprise a key set of value-category memories through which perceptions are interpreted. Edelman's concept of the "remembered present" is an apt description of flashbacks and environmentally cued intrusive memories.

As memory is linked to vital needs, it is also linked to affect. All memory has an affect charge; in effect, memory and affect come as a package. Brewer (1986) emphasized imagery as a significant component of autobiographical memory; I would put in a plug for affect. Bower (1981) elaborated the central role of affect in memory in his "semantic network" model. He described "emotion nodes" in memory as follows:

Collected around this emotion node are its associated autonomic reactions, standard role and expressive behaviors (that is, the way we display sadness), and descriptions of standard evocative situations which when appraised lead to sadness. Also included are the verbal labels commonly assigned to this emotion such as sadness, depression, and the blues. Some of these various linkages are innate, while others are learned and elaborated throughout acculturation. (p. 135)

Indeed, one's affective state at any given time can be construed as a complex amalgam based on the sum of all excited memories.

Matthysse (1991) characterized mood as the "glow of the changing pattern of memory excitation" (p. 216), elaborating as follows:

We will assume that each active memory contributes to mood qualitatively, according to the emotional quality with which it was originally invested, and quantitatively, in proportion to its moment-to-moment intensity of excitation. Mood can change for no apparent reason—we may feel irritable without provocation, or buoyant in the face of difficult odds—because the waxing and waning of the excitation of memories is largely an unconscious process. (p. 217)

Reiser (1990) has developed a similar conceptualization in the psychoanalytic context, arguing that emotion is the "glue that binds memory elements to each other, enabling those that belong together to stay together" (p. 11). In a similar vein to Bower, Reiser described memories as being organized in "nodal networks" comprising sensory percepts registered during the remembered experience and linked on the basis of their capacity to evoke the same affects. Early prototypical memories become organizers for later experience as new associations accrue in relation to shared affect. Reiser summarized that it is through connections among perception, memory, and affect that "experiences acquire meaning. That is to say that the emotional meaning of an experience could attach it to its current perceptual content and then to the past by bringing that current perceptual content into associational connection with previous emotionally meaningful experiences" (p. 124).

To recapitulate: Ordinarily, in the service of self-cohesion and adaptation more generally, perceptual experience acquires meaning by virtue of rapid, automatic, and largely unconscious integration with autobiographical memory. In the process, associated images and affects are primed; a mood is evoked. In the smooth flow of ongoing experience, autobiographical memory is continually updated by virtue of the synthesis of the "remembered present" as "my experience."

Consciousness

As we have seen, much of the synthesis of self-experience takes place automatically and unconsciously. But much else depends on active conscious integration. Indeed, consciousness is inherently integrative. Kihlstrom (1984) emphasized the role of consciousness in monitoring and controlling ourselves and our environment. Baars (1988) argued that the most fundamental adaptive function of consciousness is "the ability to support cooperative interaction between multiple knowledge sources, so as to cope with novelty" (p. 362). He construed consciousness as a "global workspace" in which such interaction can occur. Moreover, consciousness and the self are ordinarily intertwined; Baars conceptualized the self as "that which has access to consciousness" (p. 337), contending that it "provides the framework for all conscious experience" (p. 327). I think of consciousness as being on the front line, in effect, the leading edge of the active self.

Edelman (1989, 1992) made a crucial distinction between "primary consciousness," which is unreflective, immediate, and sensory, and "higher-order consciousness," which entails self-awareness as well as a capacity to link present with past and future. Higher-order consciousness does not require language but, with language and symbolization, it flourishes. Bowers (1990) made a related distinction between "first-order consciousness," referring to "noticed information" that is "selectively attended and therefore consciously perceived" (p. 145), and "second-order consciousness," which "involves beliefs, theories, and understandings of information represented in first-order consciousness" (p. 146). In a similar vein, Spiegel (1990) referred to "metaconsciousness," and Dennett (1991) proposed that there are multiple orders of consciousness (i.e., awareness of awareness of awareness to the limits of reflection).

As Bowers (1990) and Edelman (1989) implied, higher-order consciousness is the arena for dissociative processes. That is, in dissociation, the normal, meaningful integration of moment-to-moment experience (primary consciousness) does not take place (in higher-order consciousness). Spiegel (1990) made essentially the same point, viewing "consciousness as a window to parallel programs accessible to the global workspace. Self-consciousness is the awareness of processing them." In dissociation, "the experience of the window is restricted. The same number of parallel programs, perhaps five to nine, are actively sampled and processed in the global workspace, but the hypnotized individual has only one of them as an object of consciousness" (p. 131). This view is consistent with recent research suggesting that dividing attention "reduces the ability to integrate events and their context" (Craik, 1989, p. 49). Those persons with the requisite capacity to control attention can narrow the window for defensive purposes, focusing on a limited segment of experience (e.g., a sensation, an image, a fantasy) and excluding the rest, thus leaving out aspects of the self and not updating autobiography.

Ordinary discontinuity in experience

Unity and continuity in consciousness can be seen as a glass half full or half empty. As Popper's (1977) image of the airplane vapor trail implies, continuity fades over time. Short of dissociation, experience is continually punctuated with lapses in continuity (e.g., absent-mindedness), graded changes (e.g., in mood), and ego-alien states (e.g., a sense of not being "oneself"). Continuity is radically interrupted daily by sleep.

Indeed, Dennett (1991) went so far as to claim that "one of the most striking features of consciousness is its *dis*continuity—as revealed in the blind spot, and saccadic gaps, to take the simplest examples. The discontinuity of consciousness is striking because of the *apparent* continuity of consciousness" (p. 356). In a related vein, Mitchell (1991) underscored the "plural or manifold organization of self," pointing out that "we are all composites of overlapping, multiple organizations and perspectives, and our experience is smoothed over by an illusory sense of continuity" (p. 128). Spiegel's (1991) point that the continuity of experience is an *accomplishment* bears reiterating in this context. Much of the burden of this accomplishment falls on higher-order consciousness; yet higher-order consciousness is replete with fault lines for dissociation.

A simple diagram for a complex phenomenon

By now, we have left the patient far behind in the dust. How does one help the patient catch up? I find it most helpful to follow Braun (1988a, 1988b) in focusing on the *discontinuity in experience* across time. Braun's BASK model delineates four components—behavior, affect, sensation, knowledge—any or all of which may be involved in the process of dissociation. For example, hypnotic anesthesia entails a discontinuity in affect and sensation but not in behavior or knowledge, whereas emergence of an alter in multiple personality disorder entails discontinuity in all four domains. Braun's model not only enables the clinician to systematically elucidate various facets of the patient's unfolding dissociative experience (Braun, 1988b), but also provides a conceptual framework for differentiating among the various forms of dissociative disorder (Braun, 1988a).

In talking with patients about their dissociative experience, I use a highly schematic variant of Braun's model that highlights the discontinuity in their experience in stark form (see Figure 1). Continuity is represented by the solid horizontal line, discontinuity by the broken

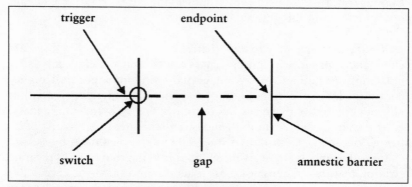

Figure 1. *Schematic model of dissociative processes.*

line in the gap. This diagram ignores various facets of experience and emphasizes five critical *junctures* in the dissociative process: triggers of dissociation, the switch process, the nature of altered experience in the gap, the endpoint, and the amnestic barrier. These five junctures also provide a useful framework for conceptualizing important aspects of dissociative processes that can be discussed with patients.

Triggers for dissociation

What triggers dissociation? Initially, dissociation is triggered by traumatic experience and overwhelming stimulation. As clinicians, we deal with the aftermath of trauma in the form of triggers in everyday life that evoke memories of trauma. Braun (1988b) has provided several instructive clinical examples of such triggers. As Minsky (1980) stated, memory is a reactivation of the state of mind/brain at the time of the remembered experience: "Each memory must embody information that can later serve to reassemble the mechanisms that were active when the memory was formed—thus recreating a 'memorable' brain event" (pp. 117-118). Ordinarily, such reactivation is partial; in flashbacks, the reactivation is more total.

As argued earlier, memory and affect are packaged together. Part and parcel of traumatic memories are fear and panic, which can be triggered in reflexlike fashion. Barlow (1991) drew on emotion theory to describe fear as "a distinct, primitive, basic emotion, or perhaps a tightly organized, cohesive affective structure stored in memory" (p. 16). He also noted the "hairtrigger, instantaneous quality of fear" and construed panic as "a normal fear response firing inappropriately" (p. 17).

The traumatized individual can be understood as having developed a "hot line" to a nodal memory network associated with fear and panic. Fear and panic may also immediately shift into rage. As Kihlstrom (1984, 1987) has described, this process unfolds unconsciously. Often, individuals feel panicky or rageful and dissociate without being aware of the cues or thoughts that evoked the traumatic memory. The activation of any part of an emotional network can rapidly activate the whole complex, all out of awareness: "We presume that an emotion is represented in memory as [a] network of information, in which response, stimulus, and meaning information are all associatively related.... Conscious evaluation is simply not a necessary part of primary emotional processing in a network theory" (Lang, 1985, p. 157). It happens unconsciously, and it happens *fast*: Long-term memories can be activated in milliseconds on the basis of stimulus fragments (Cowan, 1988).

As van der Kolk and Saporta (1991) have stated, the upshot of this unconscious processing for trauma victims is that they "go immediately from stimulus to response without being able to make the intervening psychological assessment of the cause of their arousal" (p. 202). Moreover, van der Kolk and van der Hart (1991) described how traumatic memories in particular are stored in a fashion that may preclude awareness and understanding: "The experience cannot be organized on a linguistic level and this failure to arrange the memory in words and symbols leaves it to be organized on a somatosensory or iconic level: as somatic sensations, behavioral reenactments, nightmares and flashbacks" (pp. 442-443).

Most of the trauma we deal with clinically is based in interpersonal relationships; traumatic memories are therefore primarily memories of traumatic relationship experiences. Accordingly, interpersonal interactions are prime stimuli for triggering dissociation. As Bowlby (1982) has described, we build "working models" of relationships. Horowitz (1991a) noted how individuals match these working models to earlier models of prototypical relationships, which he calls "person schemas." In effect, at any given moment in an interaction, we seek to determine, "What kind of relationship is this?" On the basis of minimal cues often operating outside awareness, traumatized individuals are liable to repeatedly construct working models that match traumatic person schemas.

The activation of traumatic relationship paradigms generates a state of emergency in the self, necessitating an extreme defense. Kluft (1992) eloquently described the threat to the self that evokes dissociative defenses:

I understand dissociation pragmatically as a defense in which an overwhelmed individual cannot escape [what] assails him or her by taking meaningful action or successful flight, and escapes instead by altering his or her internal organization; i.e., by inward flight. It is a defense of those who suffer an intolerable sense of helplessness, and have had the experience of becoming an object, the victim of someone's willful mistreatment, the indifference of nature, or of one's own limitations; one realizes that one's own will and wishes have become irrelevant to the course of events. (p. 143)

The switch process
The state of emergency in the self triggers a defensive reorganization of consciousness, an attentional shift that excludes aspects of the self from the context of experience. One of the most fascinating theoretical questions regarding dissociation is the nature of this defensive switch. Drawing on Wolff's (1987) infancy studies, Putnam (1988, 1991b) described dissociation in conjunction with changes in "behavioral

states." He regards dissociative disorders as one instance of "behavioral state disorders" associated with precipitous and radical state changes. These changes include not only flashbacks and switches in MPD but also panic states, catatonic states, and switches in bipolar disorder. Putnam (1988) defined switches as follows: "The psychobiological events associated with shifts in state of consciousness as manifest by changes in state-related variables such [as] affect, access to memories, sense of self, cognitive and perceptual style, and often reflected in alterations in facial expression, speech and motor activity, and interpersonal relatedness" (p. 26).

Putnam has meticulously studied switches in MPD, and he has also studied the time course of switches in various behavioral state disorders; he has found that they typically occur within 5 minutes from beginning to end. The concept of switching behavioral states appears to be catching on, and it has been applied by others to depression (Gilbert, 1992), Tourette syndrome (Berecz, 1992), and paranoid states (Vinogradov, King, & Huberman, 1992).

Experiences in the gap

Classifying the wide range of experiences in the gap is the task of the evolving diagnostic system (see Davidson & Foa, 1991; Gabbard, 1994; Spiegel & Cardeña, 1991, Steinberg, 1994). Thus the gap may entail trance states, depersonalization, amnesia, fugue, or emergence of alters in MPD. Experiences in the gap may also take the form of complex behavioral reenactments of dissociated traumatic events, which Blank (1985) characterized as "unconscious flashbacks." In contrast to the typical flashback, the individual is unaware of the isomorphism between the early trauma and the contemporary reenactment.

One could also picture the gap in Figure 1 as a high-amplitude sine wave, with wholesale changes in behavioral states, separated by their incompatibility. There is commonly a general polarity characterized by Spiegel (1991) as an "on-off" quality; hyperarousal (e.g., as evident in a flashback) alternates with detachment and numbing (e.g., as evident in depersonalization and derealization). Herman (1992) has aptly dubbed this oscillation the "dialectic of trauma."

Such polarized states are not only incompatible on the behavioral-experiential level, they are also incompatible on the neurophysiological level. An area of active investigation is the biochemical mediation of traumatic reactions, which appear to be hardwired. As van der Kolk and Saporta (1991) put it: "The central nervous system (CNS) seems to react to any overwhelming, threatening, and uncontrollable experience in quite a consistent pattern" (p. 201). Van der Kolk (1987, 1988, 1989; van der Kolk & Saporta, 1991) has surveyed an extensive literature on the psychophysiology of trauma and stress, which implicates (1) the activation of noradrenergic pathways from the locus ceruleus and failure of serotoninergic modulation in the hyperarousal, and (2) the activation of analgesic mechanisms associated with endogenous opioids in the numbing response.

At worst, dissociation, not continuity of experience, may be the rule (e.g., in prolonged fugues, pervasive depersonalization, or when an MPD alter is "out" for months or years). Also, there may be rapid oscillation among states associated with a sense of fragmentation and inner chaos. In this case, the gap might be pictured as a high-frequency sine wave with chaotic amplitudes. Horowitz (1991a) aptly described the state of mind associated with simultaneous activation of contradictory person schemas as "shimmering" (p. 24); this term could also apply to the chimerical experience associated with the more fragmented and complex forms of multiple personality disorder described by Kluft (1988a).

Endpoint of dissociation

An important focus for intervention is on the terminus of a dissociative state. What stops a dissociative episode? How can a therapist help a patient end such an episode (e.g., a flashback, a personality switch)? A traumatic experience is often relived, the memory replayed like a film from start to finish, in a process that is agonizing for patients and therapists alike.

It is crucial to avert retraumatization in the therapy process. As Kluft (1982) advocated, the work should be systematically paced: "It appeared most effective to proceed slowly and methodically in a very open manner, to explore resistances, respect anxieties, create an atmosphere of safety, and interrupt abrupt regressions unless the patient indicated a willingness to press ahead" (p. 234). As a general strategy for pacing therapy sessions, Kluft (1991a) proposed the "rule of thirds" (p. 178), that is, getting to the difficult work in the first third of a session, working on the difficult material in the second third, and restabilizing the patient in the final third. Kluft (1989) has described a range of temporizing techniques to help pace the therapy, such as providing sanctuary, bypassing time and affect, attenuating affect, gaining distance from memories, and reconfiguring control among alters. Kluft (1988b) has also described a "slow leak" technique for gradually diffusing affect and a painstaking process of "fractionated abreaction." These methods enable patients to master traumatic memories in tolerable doses. Fine (1991) has provided a useful summary of these pacing techniques, which enable patient and therapist to manage dissociative states with greater control.

In general, continuity is restored by forging congruity among dissociated components of experience, that is, behavior, affect, sensation, and thought (Braun, 1988b). Pragmatically, numerous techniques have evolved for "grounding" patients in current reality. These techniques have in common an intent to orient the patient back to current sensory experience. Torem (1989) has delineated several interventions, including having the patient sit up straight in a chair, blow his or her nose, get out of the room, go for a walk, take a shower, or wash his or her face; the therapist also may offer food or liquids, or turn on music.

The amnestic "barrier"

Dissociation does not end with the restoration of the state of mind prior to the trigger. It may seem as if the dissociating patient is erecting barriers against remembering or barriers among alters. "Defense" connotes a barrier thrown up—like the wall of a fortress. But a *moat* may be a better image than a wall; in dissociation, the bridges are removed. The patient avoids connections ordinarily made in higher-order consciousness; the moment-to-moment stuff of primary consciousness is left scattered, without its usual reflective synthesis in the autobiography of the self.

Baars (1988) contended that *"maintaining the self-system* may be critical for mental and physical survival" (p. 355). The traumatized self-system is maintained by markedly restricting the scope of the self:

During traumas the "I" designation, usually added to information about one's own mental or bodily experiences, may be set aside. This dissociation of self may reduce emotional reactivity. Intolerable horror or other anguish is avoided by a kind of "not me" rather than "me" designation of perceptions and memories. The dissociation may also occur because the traumatic event is so discordant with previously established schemas. (Horowitz, 1991a, p. 27)

At worst, as Fink (1988) described, dissociation can entail ruptures in the developmental foundation of the self by undermining the four cornerstones of the "core self" delineated by Stern (1985), namely, the sense of agency, coherence, affectivity, and continuity. Here, Janet's (1907) view of the dissociative phenomena in hysteria is apt: "I maintain to this day that, if hysteria is a mental malady, it is not a mental malady like any other, impairing the social sentiments or destroying the constitution of ideas. It is a malady of the *personal synthesis*" (p. 332).

MPD, the most severe dissociative disorder, evokes images of myriad internal walls and divisions. Instead, we should think of narrowly focused attention and minimal integration. Putnam (1992) warned: "The implicit and mistaken assumption made by many people is that the alter personalities are separate people. This is a serious conceptual error that will lead to therapeutic error. Alter personalities are not separate people! Rather, I think that they are best conceptualized as examples of a fundamental and discrete unit of consciousness, the behavioral state" (p. 96). In a similar vein, Kluft (1988a) protested: "How can one grapple with a 'pie' represented as divided in a hundred or a thousand portions without the metaphor becoming absurd?" (p. 56). From this vantage point, "multiple personality" is a misnomer, and Kluft tendered an alternative: "disaggregate self state disorder." He proposed that

the mind, rather than dividing itself, rather multiplies itself, recopies itself selectively, or rearranges a finite number of elements in patterns of great potential variety. It is the relatively consistent discontinuity, the relatively persistent dissociation of these copies and reconfigurations along the dimensions of memory and identity, that leads to the ongoing disaggregation of self states. (p. 57)

The core problem is not barriers but disrupted "integration of self across highly discrete states of consciousness" (Putnam, 1991a, p. 156).

The whole problem can be turned around: Rather than trying to understand how one can break apart consciousness, we can marvel at one's capacity to put it together. As Spiegel (1990) explained, "It is not remarkable that there are breaks in the continuity of personal identity ... the multiplicity of processors and occasions in which self-identity is designated, it is a complex network indeed that can integrate these disparate inputs ... and produce an apparently consistent, albeit subtly changing, self-concept" (p. 123). Indeed, "What is surprising is not that strange syndromes such as multiple personality disorder occur but rather that they do not occur more often" (p. 136). Patients in the Trauma Recovery Program of The Menninger Clinic would agree; they sometimes accuse staff members of having "single personality disorder"! The patients are in good company here; Kluft has also been alluding to "SPD" for some time (personal communication, March 25, 1993).

Dennett (1991) pushed this point to its logical conclusion: "Two or three or seventeen selves per body is really no more metaphysically extravagant than one self per body" (p. 419). Selves are (or are not) continually constructed: They are "artifacts of the social processes that create us, and, like other such artifacts, subject to sudden shifts in status. The only 'momentum' that accrues to the trajectory of a self ... is the stability imparted to it by the web of beliefs that constitute it, and when those beliefs lapse, it lapses, either permanently or temporarily"

(p. 423). Dennett summarized his understanding of the self: It is

an abstraction defined by the myriads of attributions and interpreta-
tions (including self-attributions and self-interpretations) that have
composed the biography of the living body.... As such, it plays a
singularly important role in the ongoing cognitive economy of that
living body, because, of all the things in the environment an active
body must make mental models of, none is more crucial than the
model the agent has of itself. (pp. 426-427)

To recapitulate: It is normal and adaptive to reconfigure the mind and shift among distinct behavioral states. The problem is not primarily at the level of the various states and configurations; the problem is at a higher level, namely, the inability to step back (or up) from a given state to allow higher-order consciousness to reflectively sample various states to achieve more integrated self-awareness and self-control. When life experience is abhorrent, self-construction comes to a grinding halt. Bridges are not built; moats abound.

Clinical implications

With its unintegrated and often kaleidoscopic quality, dissociative experience can be puzzling to clinicians, and it is certainly bewildering to many patients. Establishing an alliance is high on the agenda in any treatment, and it is particularly crucial in work with patients who dissociate (e.g., Braun, 1988a; Kluft, 1984, 1988a, 1991a; Putnam, 1989). As Kluft (1992) put it, "The cultivation of the therapeutic alliance is the heart and soul of the treatment of MPD" (p. 152). With these patients, establishing some shared understanding of their bewildering experience plays a key role in developing an alliance. Forming a productive diagnostic alliance can be enormously beneficial to the patient, particularly in light of the likelihood of previous misdiagnoses (Kluft, 1991b). Of course, the diagnosis must be introduced with care (Braun, 1988b), and a number of useful methods have been developed for systematically assessing patients' dissociative experiences (see Allen & Smith, 1993).

In exploring the dissociative experience of patients, I often find it helpful to make a drawing akin to the diagram in Figure 1. Once I have a feel for the nature and extent of dissociation and the patient's awareness of it, I use the diagram to explain how I think about dissociation. I also use it to help patients fill in the details of their own experience. Patients who are battling confusion related to dissociation can use a tangible focus, but they are in no mood for complicated, abstract explanations. The simplicity of the diagram helps. It immediately highlights discontinuity as a central issue. I might say, for example, "It sounds like you're going along as usual [pointing to the horizontal line on the left] and something happens. Then [pointing to the dotted line in the gap] you blank out/tune out/go far away/etc." Recognizing the irony, I ask the patient to tell me about the experience in the gap. *Something* is happening, and the patient may have at least fragmentary awareness or inferential knowledge (e.g., from evidence of past actions, or from the observations of others). Of course, finding out about gaps may also entail enabling the patient to switch states. I draw attention to the switch point (just before the left vertical) to help the patient begin thinking about triggers. And I note the importance of the endpoint (before the right vertical) to underscore the need to find ways to restore continuity (e.g., "grounding" techniques).

Just as the diagram can be useful in helping individual patients to understand and sort out their experiences, it is also useful in teaching patients in psychoeducational groups. The diagram can provide a framework for discussing common triggers, various forms of dissociative experience, grounding techniques, and amnesia. Group discussions of these aspects of dissociation enable patients to share their experiences; they learn from each other and they feel less alienated.

Either individually or in groups, a simple extension of the diagram in Figure 1 (akin to the model developed by Braun, 1988a) is useful to help patients understand the development of MPD (see Figure 2). It can be explained that repeated traumatic experience may be associated with recurrent dissociative states. For example, "Once Alice [in section A of the diagram] has discovered a way of tuning out [section B] when she is in the unbearable situation, she learns to do it whenever she needs to. After being in the altered state [section B] many times, she may experience a feeling of familiarity. As the individual develops a history of experience in that state, she may even give herself a new name, Betty, providing herself with some recognizable form of identity in that experience." Then the cascading of alters can be explained (e.g., "when

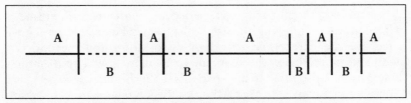

Figure 2. *Schematic representation of multiple personality disorder.*

Betty encounters an unbearable situation, she may tune out and Charlotte may evolve").

This educational and diagnostic effort in itself is therapeutic; addressing such questions invites integration and begins to expand the scope of self-experience (by appealing to higher-order consciousness). The problem is dissociation, the remedy is association (Putnam, 1991a). The problem is a "malady of personal synthesis," the remedy, self-cohesiveness. How are self-continuity and self-control restored? Janet's general strategy cannot be bettered: "Janet's difficult but successful treatment approach consisted of helping Irene restore her memories, first in hypnosis and then in the waking state. She had to translate her traumatic memories into a narrative, a personal account of the event and how it affected her personality" (van der Hart & Friedman, 1989, p. 13). As this view of treatment implies, the price of restored self-continuity is a changed identity.

The treatment of dissociative disorders is beyond the scope of this paper, and there is now an excellent body of literature available to those who endeavor to work with such patients. Here it will suffice to link the present conceptualization to current treatment strategies. To use Horowitz's (1991a) language, continuity across various states is provided by the development of "supraordinate self schemas" (p. 26) that integrate several self-schemas. Horowitz (1991b) described the integration of traumatic experiences as "a complex process that has to do in part with modifying schemas such as role relationship models so that the person's inner expectations of self as related to another will accord with new realities." This process entails that the person "bring forth different themes related to a central focus, which is how the traumatic event relates to the self" and "a new working model of what happened and its implications to the self is developed." Schematic change occurs by virtue of the formation of "schemas of schemas" that "integrate previous schemas." Crucial for the present discussion is his thesis that "by integration, some of the properties of previous schemas can be softened" (p. 169).

Putnam (1988) described the "normal developmental process that smooths out the transitions across states of consciousness" (p. 25) and emphasized that the smoothing out and modulation of disparate states is achieved through caretaking. Accordingly, trauma and a constitutional disposition to dissociate are not the only contributors to dissociative disorders; another key etiological component is the failure of caretakers to provide restorative soothing (Kluft, 1984). The *combination* of overstimulation and failure to soothe is most devastating. Much trauma could be borne if soothing were provided in its wake. Most problematic is the infliction of trauma by a caretaker. Braun (1988b) underscored the role of "untenable conflict," for example, entailed by "severe, unpredictable abuse from an otherwise *loving* mother" (p. 17). He (1990) elaborated: "While incest may be involved in child abuse that underlies MPD, the more important factor may be the unpredictable nature of the abuse. The severity of dissociation and MPD is most directly related to abuse that is administered by parents or other family members who, at other times, are able to give the child love and protection" (p. 242). Such contradictory experience sets the stage in the predisposed individual for dissociation of disparate object-relations configurations (Gabbard, 1994).

From this perspective, it should be no surprise that the mainstay of treatment for dissociative disorders is intensive, dynamically oriented psychotherapy (e.g., Braun, 1988b; Gabbard, 1994; Kluft, 1984, 1991a; Loewenstein & Ross, 1992; Marmer, 1991; Putnam, 1989). The stability of the psychotherapy relationship provides a vital "secure base" (Bowlby, 1988) and a vehicle for reestablishing the broad scope of self-experience. The result is a rewritten and expanded autobiography (Marmer, 1991).

References

Allen, J.G., & Smith, W.H. (1993). Diagnosing dissociative disorders. *Bulletin of the Menninger Clinic, 57,* 328-343.

American Psychiatric Association. (1987). *Diagnostic and statistical manual of mental disorders* (3rd ed., rev.). Washington, DC: Author.

Baars, B.J. (1988). *A cognitive theory of consciousness.* New York: Cambridge University Press.

Barlow, D.H. (1991). The nature of anxiety: Anxiety, depression, and emotional disorders. In R.M. Rapee & D.H. Barlow (Eds.), *Chronic anxiety: Generalized anxiety disorder and mixed anxiety-depression* (pp. 1-28). New York: Guilford.

Berecz, J.M. (1992). *Understanding Tourette syndrome, obsessive-compulsive disorder, and related problems: A development and catastrophe theory perspective.* New York: Springer.

Blank, A.S. (1985). The unconscious flashback to the war in Viet Nam veterans: Clinical mystery, legal defense, and community problem. In S.M. Sonnenberg, A.S. Blank, Jr., & J.A. Talbott (Eds.), *The trauma of war: Stress and recovery in Viet Nam veterans* (pp. 293-308). Washington, DC: American Psychiatric Press.

Bower, G.H. (1981). Mood and memory. *American Psychologist, 36,* 129-148.

Bowers, K.S. (1990). Unconscious influences and hypnosis. In J.L. Singer (Ed.), *Repression and dissociation: Implications for personality theory, psychopathology, and health* (pp. 143-179). Chicago: University of Chicago Press.

Bowlby, J. (1982). *Attachment and loss: Vol. 1. Attachment* (2nd ed.). New York: Basic Books.

Bowlby, J. (1988). *A secure base: Parent-child attachment and healthy human development.* New York: Basic Books.

Braun, B.G. (1988a). The BASK model of dissociation. *Dissociation, 1*(1), 4-23.

Braun, B.G. (1988b). The BASK model of dissociation: Part II–Treatment. *Dissociation, 1*(2), 16-23.

Braun, B.G. (1990). Dissociative disorders as sequelae to incest. In R.P. Kluft (Ed.), *Incest-related syndromes of adult psychopathology* (pp. 227-245). Washington, DC: American Psychiatric Press.

Braun, B.G., & Sachs, R.G. (1985). The development of multiple personality disorder: Predisposing, precipitating, and perpetuating factors. In R.P. Kluft (Ed.), *Childhood antecedents of multiple personality* (pp. 37-64). Washington, DC: American Psychiatric Press.

Brewer, W.F. (1986). What is autobiographical memory? In D.C. Rubin (Ed.), *Autobiographical memory* (pp. 25-49). New York: Cambridge University Press.

Cowan, N. (1988). Evolving conceptions of memory storage, selective attention, and their mutual constraints within the human information-processing system. *Psychological Bulletin, 104,* 163-191.

Craik, F.I.M. (1989). On the making of episodes. In H.L. Roediger III & F.I.M. Craik (Eds.), *Varieties of memory and consciousness: Essays in honor of Endel Tulving* (pp. 43-57). Hillsdale, NJ: Erlbaum.

Davidson, J.R., & Foa, E.B. (1991). Diagnostic issues in posttraumatic stress disorder: Considerations for the *DSM-IV. Journal of Abnormal Psychology, 100,* 346-355.

Dennett, D.C. (1991). *Consciousness explained.* Boston: Little, Brown.

Edelman, G.M. (1989). *The remembered present: A biological theory of consciousness.* New York: Basic Books.

Edelman, G.M. (1992). *Bright air, brilliant fire: On the matter of the mind.* New York: Basic Books.

Ellenberger, H.F. (1970). *The discovery of the unconscious: The history and evolution of dynamic psychiatry.* New York: Basic Books.

Fine, C.G. (1991). Treatment stabilization and crisis prevention: Pacing the therapy of the multiple personality disorder patient. *Psychiatric Clinics of North America, 14,* 661-675.

Fink, D.L. (1988). The core self: A developmental perspective on the dissociative disorders. *Dissociation, 1*(2), 43-47.

Gabbard, G.O. (1994). *Psychodynamic psychiatry in clinical practice: The DSM-IV edition.* Washington, DC: American Psychiatric Press.

Gilbert, P. (1992). *Depression: The evolution of powerlessness.* New York: Guilford.

Herman, J.L. (1992). *Trauma and recovery.* New York: BasicBooks.

Horowitz, M.J. (Ed.). (1991a). *Person schemas and maladaptive interpersonal patterns.* Chicago: University of Chicago Press.

Horowitz, M.J. (1991b). Short-term dynamic therapy of stress response syndromes. In P. Crits-Christoph & J.P. Barber (Eds.), *Handbook of short-term dynamic psychotherapy* (pp. 166-198). New York: Basic Books.

Janet, P. (1907). *The major symptoms of hysteria: Fifteen lectures given in the medical school of Harvard University.* New York: Macmillan.

Kihlstrom, J.F. (1984). Conscious, subconscious, unconscious: A cognitive perspective. In K.S. Bowers & D. Meichenbaum (Eds.), *The unconscious reconsidered* (pp. 149-211). New York: Wiley.

Kihlstrom, J.F. (1987). The cognitive unconscious. *Science, 237,* 1445-1452.

Kihlstrom, J.F., & Hoyt, I.P. (1990). Repression, dissociation, and hypnosis. In J.L. Singer (Ed.), *Repression and dissociation: Implications for personality theory, psychopathology, and health* (pp. 181-208). Chicago: University of Chicago Press.

Kluft, R.P. (1982). Varieties of hypnotic interventions in the treatment of multiple personality. *American Journal of Clinical Hypnosis, 24,* 230-240.

Kluft, R.P. (1984). Treatment of multiple personality disorder: A study of 33 cases. *Psychiatric Clinics of North America, 7,* 9-29.

Kluft, R.P. (1988a). The phenomenology and treatment of extremely complex multiple personality disorder. *Dissociation, 1*(4), 47-58.

Kluft, R.P. (1988b). On treating the older patient with multiple personality disorder: "Race against time" or "make haste slowly?" *American Journal of Clinical Hypnosis, 30,* 257-266.

Kluft, R.P. (1989). Playing for time: Temporizing techniques in the treatment of multiple personality disorder. *American Journal of Clinical Hypnosis, 32,* 90-98.

Kluft, R.P. (1991a). Multiple personality disorder. In A. Tasman & S.M. Goldfinger (Eds.), *American Psychiatric Press review of psychiatry* (Vol. 10, pp. 161-188). Washington, DC: American Psychiatric Press.

Kluft, R.P. (1991b). Clinical presentations of multiple personality disorder. *Psychiatric Clinics of North America, 14,* 605-629.

Kluft, R.P. (1992). Discussion: A specialist's perspective on multiple personality disorder. *Psychoanalytic Inquiry, 12,* 139-171.

Kohut, H. (1979). Four basic concepts in self psychology. In P.H. Ornstein (Ed.), *The search for the self: Selected writings of Heinz Kohut: 1978-1981* (pp. 447-470). Madison, CT: International Universities Press.

Kuhn, T.S. (1962). *The structure of scientific revolutions.* Chicago: University of Chicago Press.

Lang, P.J. (1985). The cognitive psychophysiology of emotion: Fear and anxiety. In A.H. Tuma & J. Maser (Eds.), *Anxiety and the anxiety disorders* (pp. 131-170). Hillsdale, NJ: Erlbaum.

Loewenstein, R.J., & Ross, D.R. (1992). Multiple personality and psychoanalysis: An introduction. *Psychoanalytic Inquiry, 12,* 3-48.

Marmer, S.S. (1991). Multiple personality disorder: A psychoanalytic perspective. *Psychiatric Clinics of North America, 14,* 677-693.

Matthysse, S. (1991). Mood disorders and the dynamic stability of the system of memories. In J. Madden IV (Ed.), *Neurobiology of learning, emotion and affect* (pp. 215-228). New York: Raven Press.

Minsky, M. (1980). K-lines: A theory of memory. *Cognitive Science, 4,* 117-133.

Mitchell, S.A. (1991). Contemporary perspectives on self: Toward an integration. *Psychoanalytic Dialogues, 1,* 121-147.

Perry, C., & Laurence, J. (1984). Mental processing outside of awareness: The contributions of Freud and Janet. In K.S. Bowers & D. Meichenbaum (Eds.), *The unconscious reconsidered* (pp. 9-48). New York: Wiley.

Popper, K.R. (1977). Some remarks on the self. In K.R. Popper & J.C. Eccles, *The self and its brain* (pp. 100-147). New York: Springer International.

Putnam, F.W. (1988). The switch process in multiple personality disorder and other state-change disorders. *Dissociation, 1*(1), 24-32.

Putnam, F.W. (1989). *Diagnosis and treatment of multiple personality disorder.* New York: Guilford.

Putnam, F.W. (1991a). Dissociative phenomena. In A. Tasman & S.M. Goldfinger (Eds.), *American Psychiatric Press review of psychiatry* (Vol. 10, 145-160). Washington, DC: American Psychiatric Press.

Putnam, F.W. (1991b). Recent research on multiple personality disorder. *Psychiatric Clinics of North America, 14,* 489-502.

Putnam, F.W. (1992). Discussion: Are alter personalities fragments or figments? *Psychoanalytic Inquiry, 12,* 95-111.

Reiser, M.F. (1990). *Memory in mind and brain: What dream imagery reveals.* New York: Basic Books.

Schacter, D.L. (1989). Memory. In M.I. Posner (Ed.), *Foundations of cognitive science* (pp. 683-725). Cambridge: MIT Press.

Spiegel, D. (1988). Dissociation and hypnosis in post-traumatic stress disorders. *Journal of Traumatic Stress, 1,* 17-33.

Spiegel, D. (1990). Hypnosis, dissociation, and trauma: Hidden and overt observers. In J.L. Singer (Ed.), *Repression and dissociation: Implications for personality theory, psychopathology, and health* (pp. 121-142). Chicago: University of Chicago Press.

Spiegel, D. (1991). Foreword. In A. Tasman & S.M. Goldfinger (Eds.), *American Psychiatric Press review of psychiatry* (Vol. 10, pp. 143-144). Washington, DC: American Psychiatric Press.

Spiegel, D., & Cardeña, E. (1991). Disintegrated experience: The dissociative disorders revisited. *Journal of Abnormal Psychology, 100,* 366-378.

Steinberg, M. (1994). Systematizing dissociation: Symptomatology and diagnostic assessment. In D. Spiegel (Ed.), *Dissociation: Culture, mind and body* (pp. 59-88). Washington, DC: American Psychiatric Press.

Stern, D.N. (1985). *The interpersonal world of the infant: A view from psychoanalysis and developmental psychology.* New York: Basic Books.

Torem, M.S. (1989). Recognition and management of dissociative regressions. *Hypnos, 16,* 197-213.

van der Hart, O., & Friedman, B. (1989). A reader's guide to Pierre Janet on dissociation: A neglected intellectual heritage. *Dissociation, 2,* 3-16.

van der Kolk, B. (1987). *Psychological trauma.* Washington, DC: American Psychiatric Press.

van der Kolk, B.A. (1988). The trauma spectrum: The interaction of biological and social events in the genesis of the trauma response. *Journal of Traumatic Stress, 1,* 273-290.

van der Kolk, B.A. (1989). The compulsion to repeat the trauma: Re-enactment, revictimization, and masochism. *Psychiatric Clinics of North America, 12,* 389-411.

van der Kolk, B.A., & Saporta, J. (1991). The biological response to psychic trauma: Mechanisms and treatment of intrusion and numbing. *Anxiety Research, 4,* 199-212.

van der Kolk, B.A., & van der Hart, O. (1991). The intrusive past: The flexibility of memory and the engraving of trauma. *American Imago, 48,* 425-454.

Vinogradov, S., King, R.J., & Huberman, B.A. (1992). An associationist model of the paranoid process: Application of phase transitions in spreading activation networks. *Psychiatry, 55,* 79-94.

Wolff, P.H. (1987). *The development of behavioral states and the expression of emotions in early infancy: New proposals for investigation.* Chicago: University of Chicago Press.

Young, W.C. (1988). Psychodynamics and dissociation: All that switches is not split. *Dissociation, 1*(1), 33-38.

2. Toward a Psychoanalytic Understanding of Multiple Personality Disorder

Bruce E. Reis, PhD

The author suggests a developmental psychoanalytic frame from which to understand the clinical phenomenology of multiple personality disorder (MPD). Annihilation anxiety and fears of nonbeing are understood as central; they are seen as resulting from actual early traumatic impingements at key developmental periods. Alter "personalities" are conceptualized as functional delusional processes that serve to maintain self-cohesion. The alters are brought about through the subject's lack of capacity for illusion. Some therapeutic implications regarding a psychoanalytic stance are discussed.

The past decade has seen tremendous growth in the literature describing childhood traumatization and the development of dissociative and multiple personality disorders (MPD). Seminal texts and papers (e.g., Putnam, 1989; van der Kolk, 1987) as well as an entire journal, *Dissociation* (launched in 1988), have marked the surge of interest in the study of these phenomena. Although it is beyond the scope of this paper to provide an inclusive review of this burgeoning literature, which with poor boundedness has come to be known as "the trauma literature," I will present a selective primer to illustrate areas of contrast and commonalities with psychoanalytic work in this area.

Kluft's (1984, 1988) "four factor theory" summarizes current thinking regarding the etiological factors that are thought to contribute to the formation of MPD. This complex interactive model involves: (1) biological predisposition to dissociation; (2) exposure to overwhelming trauma; (3) the influence of mediating "shaping factors"; and (4) unavailability of soothing, absence of protection from additional traumatization, and lack of opportunity to process and metabolize the traumatic material. These factors are believed to constitute the conditions for the development of MPD.

Kluft (1992) observed that in contemporary American society, exogenous traumatic stressors are likely to be instances of child abuse, which has been reported by 97-98% of patients with MPD (Putnam,

An earlier version of this article was presented in June 1993 at a conference in Boston on "Psychological Trauma: Maturational Processes and Therapeutic Interventions," sponsored by Harvard Medical School. Dr. Reis is a staff psychologist at the Trauma Clinic of Massachusetts General Hospital and Harvard Medical School.

Guroff, Silberman, Barban, & Post, 1986; Schultz, Braun, & Kluft, 1989). Such abuse often begins early in life (Ross et al., 1990). As Loewenstein and Ross (1992) described:

The new paradigm of MPD states that it is a complex, chronic form of developmental posttraumatic dissociative disorder, primarily related to severe, repetitive childhood abuse or trauma, usually beginning before the age of five. In MPD, it is thought that dissociative defenses are used to protect the child from the full psychological impact of severe trauma, usually extreme, repetitive child abuse. (p. 7)

In this understanding, the development of dissociative defenses and alter personalities is seen as an adaptive, normative reaction to experiences of extreme trauma. Dissociation continues to function in the service of separating traumatic experiences (in the form of "This is not happening to me, it is happening to someone else"), allowing the individual to function at sometimes remarkably high levels, although at an internal cost. Dissociative symptoms include depersonalization and derealization. Frequent and prolonged amnestic periods produce subjective experiences of discontinuities in experience.

Although Loewenstein and Ross (1992) observed that the intrapsychic symptomatology of MPD often includes internal auditory hallucinations (the voices of alter personalities), thought insertion and withdrawal, vivid alterations in perception such as visual and olfactory hallucinations, and varying degrees of loss of contact with and orientation to contemporary reality, they strictly regard these changes as posttraumatic sequelae and not as a "true process thought disorder" (p. 19). Posttraumatic sequelae also include reexperiencing phenomena such as flashbacks and "body memories," as well as other intrusive recollections that lead the individual to feel as if he or she were reliving the traumatic events.

A psychoanalytic perspective on multiple personality disorder

Psychoanalytic descriptions of patients with MPD stretch back to the influence of Janet and Breuer on Freud's early writings about the disorder, and to Fairbairn's later contributions (Berman, 1981). Several current analytic authors (Davies & Frawley, 1992a, 1992b; Loewenstein & Ross, 1992; Simon, 1992) have reviewed the uneasy tension that psychoanalysis has traditionally experienced concerning the influence of external trauma on the development of the inner world of the patient. According to these reviews, the psychoanalytic literature has historically regarded dissociation as a defense mechanism embedded in a classical drive theory model of psychic functioning. As such, MPD has traditionally been understood in an id-superego conflict model involving forbidden wishes and fantasies of an oedipal nature. Simon's (1992) wryly titled paper, for instance, resulted from his discovery that under "Incest" in the index of Fenichel's (1945) *The Psychoanalytic Theory of Neurosis,* the reader is directed to "See under Oedipus Complex."

As the statistics cited earlier on the prevalence of child sexual abuse become known within the analytic community, the etiological role of early, severe, malignant psychological abuse and torture is being more widely incorporated into contemporary psychoanalytic understanding of multiple personality (e.g., Marmer, 1991). The growing recognition that traumatic injury often occurs early in life focuses increasing attention on issues of developmental arrest.

Object relations theory

Building on earlier work of the British object relations school, a psychoanalytic knowledge base is forming from which to understand the psychic transformations brought on through early severe trauma. Brief case material is presented here to illustrate the applicability of theory to the clinical phenomenology of MPD.

The archaic beginnings of child sexual abuse are dramatically related by one MPD patient's report of abuse that occurred at the preverbal level, prior to the adequate formation of a symbolic capacity: "My father started sexually abusing me before I had words." This importance of a synthetic symbolizing function has been noted to be pivotal in the processing of traumatic experience (Ducey & van der Kolk, 1991). In the absence of these operations—due perhaps to the immaturity of the psychic apparatus—affect remains unintegrated and unmodulated by higher cognitive processes, and experience is not synthesized. Bollas (1992) remarked that "children whose parents are impinging or acutely traumatizing collect such trauma into an internal psychic area which is intended to bind and limit the damage to the self, even though it will nucleate into an increasingly sophisticated internal complex as resonant trauma are unconsciously 'referred' to such an area for linked containment" (p. 69). As this complex develops over time, it is subject to the influence of fantasy as well as secondary process elaboration.

The importance of the early developmental stage at which many of these patients experienced traumatic insult cannot be underestimated in understanding their self-development, and in understanding the frequent narratives of murders and other occurrences during satanic cult ritual practices that these adult patients relate (see Sakheim & Devine, 1992). At the infantile stage during which actual traumatic insults began, key psychic boundaries (e.g., between self and other) had not yet been fully developed, reality and fantasy not yet securely established.

Tracey (1991) noted that in normal development, Bion (1977) described the use of projective identification not as a defense but as a mode of communication "by which the infant lets the mother know what he is feeling. Thus the feeling, known, shared and divested of its fear by the containing mother, is made tolerable and can be kept" (Tracey, 1991, p. 32). With trauma comes the failure of containment and the inability to process these projections. Harris (1970/1987) suggested that such environmental failure "results in the introjection of an object that is hostile to understanding, together with the frightened part of himself which is divested of meaning through not eliciting a response. This is then experienced as a nameless dread" (p. 142). It is interesting to conceptualize the formation of what will later be experienced as discrete alter personalities in this process of failed containment, fragmentation of the maternal object, and reintrojection of the annihilating object originally described by Bion (1962). The difference suggested here is that actual traumatic impingements are believed to have occurred; this process is not merely derivative of the vicissitudes of the death instinct as first held by Klein (1946/1975a). Significantly, such an understanding gives primary importance to the developing intersubjective context in which the patient's difficulties arose. Grotstein (1991) observed that this distinction was clearly recognized by the Independent wing of the British school (e.g., Fairbairn, Winnicott, Balint).

During normal development, the presymbolic child may flourish in the area Winnicott (1971) referred to as "potential space," an intermediate area between reality and fantasy. This area results from a successfully negotiated process of separation from the maternal object, and it is the source of symbolic thought, play, and cultural experience (B.L. Smith, 1989). It is also the area that serves as the basis for the ontological foundation of the subject (Usuelli, 1992). Where separation has been traumatic, or where maternal care has been too inconsistent, the experience of "primitive agony" (Winnicott, 1974, p. 104) fills this space.

Building on the illustration of these processes, Ogden (1989a) suggested a dialectical process between reality and fantasy in which each creates and negates the other, and in which neither concept has meaning except in relationship with the other. According to Ogden, disruptions of this interplay within the potential space may result in dissociation of each pole from the other, a resulting loss of meaning, and a collapse of potential space.

B.L. Smith (1990) conceived of dissociative disorders as a form of collapsed potential space, in which reality and fantasy are experienced as parallel but disconnected realities. According to B.L. Smith (1989), the patient with multiple personality disorder has failed to achieve and use transitional object phenomena at a phase-appropriate time; consequently, fantasy objects are experienced not as illusory but as real, or, in Winnicott's (1969) terms, as found rather than created. According to Smith, this lack of capacity for illusion is what gives the alter personalities their reality.

A lack of capacity for illusion, resulting from gaps in the potential space, has been credited (Usuelli, 1992) with preventing the individual from making sense of personal experience, from feeling those experiences as real. When this failure occurs, delusional ideas rush in to fill the gap in the structure of the transitional space. Where psychic reality has been endangered by traumatic impingements, delusion formation has been seen (Stolorow, Brandchaft, & Atwood, 1987) as a restorative attempt to concretize, substantialize, and preserve a reality that has begun to disintegrate. Such delusions serve as a defense against annihilation, protecting the individual from the threat of dissolution.

Ontological issues

I conceptualize the core difficulty experienced by severely disordered multiple personality patients as one with *ontological* dimensions, brought on by the collapse of potential space. Clinical support for linking an impairment in symbolic thinking with collapsed potential space has been noted in the inability of patients who were sexually abused as children to maintain the "as if" quality of the transference (Bollas, 1989; Levine, 1990) and in the inability of children who have been traumatized to engage in symbolic play (Terr, 1981).

Collapse of the early potential space results in the concretization of personality fragments experienced as actual (separate personalities). Although these fragments are often regarded as pieces of the host or executive personality, they are more correctly regarded as narrative constructions, as seen for instance in the not uncommon phenomenon of animal alter personalities (e.g., S.G. Smith, 1989). These may be best understood, I believe, not as structures or alter personalties, but as functional delusional processes whose aim is to maintain self-cohesiveness.

For example, the adolescent male alter of a 30-year-old female patient with MPD analyzed the defensive/adaptive function of "his" existence in the avoidance of emotional trauma and massive anxiety. In speaking with this alter in therapy, I had learned that "he" was responsible for much of the mutilative cutting of the genitals and breasts that was occurring between sessions. Discussion with this alter revealed the delusional belief that if the cut was deep enough or in just the right place, a penis would eventually be discovered, proving "he" was a boy. Being a boy was "safer," in the logic of this alter, because there are fewer ways to be sexually violated. In a remarkable admission, this alter commented about knowing that "he" was a girl and not a boy. Being a girl, however, aroused feelings of terror at abuse, because being a girl is associated with the experience of repeated forced vaginal penetration.

In adopting the false self of being a boy rather than integrating the dissociated or split-off affect, this patient illustrates how the "personalities" in MPD may serve as functional processes in the psychic containment of affect. This patient's presentation is similar to Pierre Janet's turn-of-the-century formulation of the multiple personality patient's "successive existences" (Loewenstein & Ross, 1992, p. 30), as well as to Kluft's (1994) current reconceptualization of MPD as a "multiple reality disorder." With insight, this patient moved toward awareness of a totality of her own experience, supplying meaning and re-creating the dialectical process between reality and fantasy (i.e., the patient understood the alter personality as illusory). In the patient's analysis of the defensive/adaptive processes, warded-off areas of self-experience (affects, fantasies, fears) were ultimately recovered, and the ego resumed its process of synthesis.

The self that is experienced as fragmented and encapsulated into bits and pieces has been seen as a defense against annihilation anxiety and associated with early traumatization (Hopper, 1991). At a core level, the basic struggle of these severely disordered MPD patients is with fear of nonbeing or "de-real-'I'-zation," which characterizes their psychic life. Marmer (1991) compared this annihilating force to

the way these patients as children experienced their parents and their lives. In childhood, many of these patients experienced a parent who was good at one time changing into a parent who was unspeakably bad at another time. They survived this change in the parent by changing themselves. At such a time, the extreme method of dissociation is like a mini-annihilation from which it is possible to return. Out of this comes the belief that one can be annihilated, as well as die, and then return to life again. Confusion between the two concepts may develop. (p. 682)

Marmer noted that the many reports these patients give of deaths, disappearances, and killings (both internal and external) may be informed by an understanding of these central fears about ontological issues. I believe that this explanation is true and would add that, taken together with the Kleinian concept of the cannibalistic annihilation of internal objects by the infant (Muensterberger, 1978), there is a considerable theory base from which to conceive of these difficulties psychoanalytically. The memories of cannibalistic cult activity commonly reported by MPD patients may constitute a delusional production in which the consumed infant represents the patient's own annihilation anxiety, which has been dissociated in another "not me" experience.

Within the paranoid-schizoid mode of experiencing (Klein, 1946/ 1975a, 1958/1975b), there exists almost no space between the symbol and the symbolized. Ogden (1989b) held that the absence of the capacity to symbolically mediate between oneself and one's experience engenders a quite limited form of subjectivity. In the paranoid-schizoid position, "the self is to a large extent a self-as-object, a self that only minimally experiences itself as the author of its own thoughts, feelings, sensations, and perceptions" (p. 53). This description is consistent with one MPD patient's memory of having been treated "like an object, with no feelings" when she was a child, which is how she psychically transformed parts of her self. The similarity between this mode of experience and the descriptions of alter and dissociative "not-me" experience is strikingly familiar to clinicians working with such patients. In fact, some 50 years ago, Fairbairn (1944) recognized the dissociative phenomena described by Janet as "fundamentally identical" (p. 74) to the mode of experiencing in Klein's paranoid-schizoid position. Most of what is currently considered posttraumatic reliving sequelae can also be understood as occurring within this mode.

Severe dissociative states have been noted, however, which are understood to represent a total cessation in the process of attributing meaning to experience. These states are also seen as a regression to Ogden's (1989b) controversial autistic-contiguous position (Gabbard, 1992). Interestingly, several authors (Gabbard, 1992; Tracey, 1991) have referred to these severe dissociative states as a "psychological deadness" (Gabbard, 1992, p. 44) in which the patient appears unresponsive to the analyst's attempts at contact. One patient with MPD referred to these latter experiences as falling into a "black hole," a term also used by Grotstein (1983) to describe a similar autistic psychic space in which meaning is obliterated. We may conceive of these psychic spaces as gaps in the potential space that have been annihilated as a result of trauma, and that have not been modified through the influx of delusion.

Examples of the struggle with issues of "being" and reality involve the often-cited (e.g., Kluft, 1994) clinical presentation of these patients with what may be termed a chronically acute suicidality, as well as with a verbalized desire to self-mutilate as a way to make psychic pain—in the words of one woman—"real." The pain experienced through cutting may also serve to renew boundaries between the external and the internal world, lessening the threat of disintegration by providing the sensation, although painful, of being held together by the skin barrier in a manner similar to that described by Bick (1968). At the level of the skin ego, this pain is the most basic form of experiencing reality at a presymbolic level and of battling the feelings of "deadness" described by so many mutilators who have been sexually abused (van der Kolk, Perry, & Herman, 1991).

Therapeutic implications

The essential goal of the treatment relationship is to establish for the patient an experience of feeling cared for and understood by another person, without the attendant pain and terror that precipitated annihilation anxiety in the past. Conversely, part of this goal is to demonstrate through the containment and holding functions of the relationship that the patient's affects may be held in the relationship, then processed and reintrojected as tolerable affective experience. As a "continuity of being" (Winnicott, 1960, p. 594) takes hold, the subject is thus ushered further into existence (as in the clinical case example presented earlier). For this development to occur within the therapeutic frame, the therapist must "maintain dual citizenship in two domains of reality, with passports to multiple self-states of the patient" (Bromberg, 1991, p. 410) without losing his or her own subjectivity and without simply reifying the patient's. Bromberg (1991) cogently observed that such patients do not need to be corrected on their faulty perception of reality; rather, they require an empathic relationship with another person through which their as yet unsymbolized experiences may find expression.

These patients are often invested in their diagnosis because it serves an important role in maintaining a narcissistic identification as a multiple personality disorder individual. Such an identity gives narrative structure to chaotic, traumatic experience and should be challenged with great care. As B.L. Smith (1989) correctly noted, in the midst of the false-self adaptations that these patients have had to develop to survive intolerable life circumstances, the true self exists only as a potentiality. Its emergence must therefore be facilitated with therapeutic sensitivity.

To the extent that the work of the British school of object relations has been overlooked in current clinical investigations of multiple personality, researchers will continue to rediscover clinical phenomena that treaters struggled with half a century ago. Likewise, to the degree that modern psychoanalytic thought can incorporate the scientific data as well as the humane approach of the trauma-focused group, new understanding of our patients will become available, which we may then bring into the intersubjective context of treatment. Where childhood sexual abuse has occurred, this paper suggests forms for intrapsychic transformations in MPD and the particular applicability of the work of the British object relations school to the clinical material described in the trauma literature.

References

Berman, E. (1981). Multiple personality: Psychoanalytic perspectives. *International Journal of Psycho-Analysis, 62,* 283-300.

Bick, E. (1968). The experience of the skin in early object-relations. *International Journal of Psycho-Analysis, 49,* 484-486.

Bion, W.R. (1962). *Learning from experience.* New York: Basic Books.

Bion, W.R. (1977). *Seven servants.* New York: Aronson.

Bollas, C. (1989). *Forces of destiny: Psychoanalysis and human idiom.* Northvale, NJ: Aronson.

Bollas, C. (1992). *Being a character: Psychoanalysis and self experience.* New York: Hill and Wang.

Bromberg, P.M. (1991). On knowing one's patient inside out: The aesthetics of unconscious communication. *Psychoanalytic Dialogues, 1,* 399-422.

Davies, J.M., & Frawley, M.G. (1992a). Dissociative processes and transference-countertransference paradigms in the psychoanalytically oriented treatment of adult survivors of childhood sexual abuse. *Psychoanalytic Dialogues, 2,* 5-36.

Davies, J.M., & Frawley, M.G. (1992b). Reply to Gabbard, Shengold, and Grotstein. *Psychoanalytic Dialogues, 2,* 77-96.

Ducey, C.P., & van der Kolk, B.A. (1991). The psychological processing of traumatic experience: Reply to Cohen and de Ruiter. *Journal of Traumatic Stress, 4,* 425-432.

Fairbairn, W.R.D. (1944). Endopsychic structure considered in terms of object-relationships. *International Journal of Psycho-Analysis, 25,* 70-93.

Fenichel, O. (1945). *The psychoanalytic theory of neurosis.* New York: Norton.

Gabbard, G.O. (1992). Commentary on "Dissociative processes and transference-countertransference paradigms in the psychoanalytically oriented treatment of adult survivors of childhood sexual abuse." *Psychoanalytic Dialogues, 2,* 37-47.

Grotstein, J.S. (1983). [Book review of *Autistic states in childhood*]. *International Review of Psycho-Analysis, 10,* 491-498.

Grotstein, J.S. (1991). Commentary on "Dissociative processes and transference-countertransference paradigms in the psychoanalytically oriented treatment of adult survivors of childhood sexual abuse." *Psychoanalytic Dialogues, 2,* 61-76.

Harris, M. (1987). Some notes on maternal containment in good enough mothering. In M. Harris-Williams (Ed.), *Collected papers of Martha Harris and Esther Bick* (pp. 141-163). Strath Tay, Scotland: Clunie. (Original work published 1970)

Hopper, E. (1991). Encapsulation as a defence against the fear of annihilation. *International Journal of Psycho-Analysis, 72,* 607-624.

Klein, M. (1975a). Notes on some schizoid mechanisms. In *Envy and gratitude and other works, 1946-1963* (pp.1-24). New York: Free Press. (Original work published 1946)

Klein, M. (1975b). On the development of mental functioning. In *Envy and gratitude and other works, 1946-1963* (pp. 236-246). New York: Free Press. (Original work published 1958)

Kluft, R.P. (1984). Aspects of the treatment of multiple personality disorder. *Psychiatric Annals, 14*, 51-55.

Kluft, R.P. (1988). The dissociative disorders. In J.A. Talbott, R.E. Hales, & S.C. Yudofsky (Eds.), *American Psychiatric Press textbook of psychiatry* (pp. 557-585). Washington, DC: American Psychiatric Press.

Kluft, R.P. (1992). A specialist's perspective on multiple personality disorder. *Psychoanalytic Inquiry, 12*, 139-171.

Kluft, R.P. (1994). Countertransference in the treatment of multiple personality disorder. In J.P. Wilson & J.D. Lindy (Eds.), *Countertransference and the treatment of PTSD* (pp. 122-206). New York: Guilford.

Levine, H.B. (Ed.). (1990). *Adult analysis and childhood sexual abuse*. Hillsdale, NJ: Analytic Press.

Loewenstein, R.J., & Ross, D.R. (1992). Multiple personality and psychoanalysis: An introduction. *Psychoanalytic Inquiry, 12*, 3-48.

Marmer, S.S. (1991). Multiple personality disorder: A psychoanalytic perspective. *Psychiatric Clinics of North America, 14*, 677-693.

Muensterberger, W. (1978). Between reality and fantasy. In S.A. Grolnick & L. Barkin (Eds.), *Between reality and fantasy: Transitional objects and phenomena* (pp. 5-13). New York: Aronson.

Ogden, T.H. (1989a). Playing, dreaming, and interpreting experience: Comments on potential space. In M.G. Fromm & B.L. Smith (Eds.), *The facilitating environment: Clinical applications of Winnicott's theory* (pp. 255-278). Madison, CT: International Universities Press.

Ogden, T.H. (1989b). *The primitive edge of experience*. Northvale, NJ: Aronson.

Putnam, F.W. (1989). *Diagnosis and treatment of multiple personality disorder*. New York: Guilford.

Putnam, F.W., Guroff, J.J., Silberman, E.K., Barban, L., & Post, R.M. (1986). The clinical phenomenology of multiple personality disorder: Review of 100 recent cases. *Journal of Clinical Psychiatry, 47*, 285-293.

Ross, C.A., Miller, S.D., Reagor, P., Bjornson, L., Fraser, G.A., & Anderson, G. (1990). Structured interview data on 102 cases of multiple personality disorder from four centers. *American Journal of Psychiatry, 147*, 596-601.

Sakheim, D.K., & Devine, S.E. (1992). *Out of darkness: Exploring satanism and ritual abuse*. New York: Lexington Books.

Schultz, R., Braun, B.G., & Kluft, R.P. (1989). Multiple personality disorder: Phenomenology of selected variables in comparison to major depression. *Dissociation, 2*, 45-51.

Simon, B. (1992). "Incest. See under Oedipus Complex": The history of an error in psychoanalysis. *Journal of the American Psychoanalytic Association, 40*, 955-988.

Smith, B.L. (1989). Of many minds: A contribution on the dynamics of multiple personality. In M.G. Fromm & B.L. Smith (Eds.), *The facilitating environment: Clinical applications of Winnicott's theory* (pp. 424-458). Madison, CT: International Universities Press.

Smith, B.L. (1990). Potential space and the Rorschach: An application of object relations theory. *Journal of Personality Assessment, 55*, 756-767.

Smith, S.G. (1989). Multiple personalty disorder with human and non-human subpersonality components. *Dissociation, 2*, 52-56.

Stolorow, R.D., Brandchaft, B., & Atwood, G.E. (1987). *Psychoanalytic treatment: An intersubjective approach*. Hillsdale, NJ: Analytic Press.

Terr, L.C. (1981). Forbidden games: Post-traumatic child's play. *Journal of the American Academy of Child Psychiatry, 20*, 741-760.

Tracey, N. (1991). The psychic space in trauma. *Journal of Child Psychotherapy,* *17*(2), 29-43.

Usuelli, A.K. (1992). The significance of illusion in the work of Freud and Winnicott: A controversial issue. *International Review of Psycho-Analysis, 19,* 179-187.

van der Kolk, B.A. (1987). *Psychological trauma.* Washington, DC: American Psychiatric Press.

van der Kolk, B.A., Perry, J.C., & Herman, J.L. (1991). Childhood origins of self-destructive behavior. *American Journal of Psychiatry, 148,* 1665-1671.

Winnicott, D. W. (1960). The theory of the parent-infant relationship. *International Journal of Psycho-Analysis, 41,* 585-595.

Winnicott, D.W. (1969). The use of an object. *International Journal of Psycho-Analysis, 50,* 711-716.

Winnicott, D.W. (1971). *Playing and reality.* London: Tavistock.

Winnicott, D.W. (1974). Fear of breakdown. *International Review of Psycho-Analysis, 1,* 103-107.

3. Selves That Starve and Suffocate: The Continuum of Eating Disorders and Dissociative Phenomena

Kathryn J. Zerbe, MD

Recent reports suggest a link between eating disorders and dissociative phenomena. The author offers a psychodynamic perspective on this connection and proposes that these disorders may occur along a continuum. Viewing these conditions as related suggests that eating disorders, like dissociative disorders, may have not only self-destructive but also self-preserving aspects. The author explores treatment implications of this perspective.

In 1907 Pablo Picasso completed the painting *Les Demoiselles d'Avignon.* Ushering in the Cubist period, this polemic work recasts the depiction of the classic female nude; it radically fractures and distorts the physical body. No longer is woman drawn as rounded, unfolding, comforting, knowable, and inviting. Now she appears fragmented and split apart, with many angular, distorted, monstrous features composing her visage. In this painting, woman does not know herself and we cannot know her. Her body parts are wedded together as if in a paper collage, giving the appearance of a twisted, deformed torso incapable of synchronous, normal action. The five women depicted might be construed as five perspectives of the same person—five aspects of the ineffable self. This painting appeals to our inner sense of disconnection and dissonance. We identify with how the part may represent the whole, with the mask that hides the real face. We study the arms, legs, and faces, struck by how our own physique may sometimes appear or feel alien to us. The painting reminds us that many parts of ourselves remain unknowable, or unfathomable, even as we are always attempting to pull together many perplexing, often contradictory, aspects of our personality.

Surely most humans have at least occasionally been caught off guard by the daily encounters where different sides of the personality speak. Have you ever been talking behind a friend's back? Suddenly, you turn around and see the person appear at your door. Your attitude makes an abrupt about-face. You become pleasant, even kind. Later you may find yourself wondering what transpired between the moment of your earlier

This article is based on a presentation at a Menninger Continuing Education conference, "Dissociative States: Multiple Personality and Other Trauma-Related Disorders," held February 14-16, 1992, at Topeka, Kansas. Dr. Zerbe is vice president for Education, Research, and Applications at The Menninger Clinic.

ad hominem critique and your later embracing, welcoming mode. Were you just exerting a modicum of social charm and personal flexibility, able to meet the social demand as the occasion arose? Or was your experience of yourself more deceptive than meets the eye? How would you know if these were two very dichotomous states of your personality being manifested at different moments—what some have called, in the professional and lay literature, alter selves or personalities?

Perhaps one test of the integration of self comes from how consciously we hold varying perspectives of ourselves and other people in full awareness from moment to moment. The more easily we do this, the better we seem to know ourselves and the more we experience self-cohesion. Yet we must be cautious. Experiences like the one I have just described can often be disconcerting. From time to time, even the most well-adjusted and knowledgeable individuals ask why and under what circumstances they see different aspects of themselves emerge. Temporarily losing our temper, feeling overwhelmed with anxiety as we contemplate an upcoming speech, or feigning interest in the subject of a friend's conversation when we really are quite disdainful and mentally far away—these situations are just a few examples of the fluidity of the self-experience. However briefly you experience the gaffe, you may be said to temporarily lose the experience of knowing yourself. Yet these discomforting moments that all of us encounter in daily life make us more cognizant of and empathic toward the much deeper rifts in self-continuity that our patients with dissociative disorders valiantly struggle against.

To be sure, the burgeoning literature on multiple personality disorder (MPD) and dissociative states (Kluft, 1987, 1991a, 1991b) has propelled numerous investigators to reconsider the nature of the autonomous self (Sutherland, 1993). The appreciation of these diagnoses has not only led clinicians to suggest a variety of therapeutic techniques to treat such patients (Davies & Frawley, 1992; Kluft, 1992; Ogden, 1991), but it has also raised many questions about our understanding of phenomena witnessed almost daily on any hospital unit and in outpatient practice (Kluft, 1991b). The field is still in its infancy in ascertaining what precisely occurs in the brain to engender and then perpetuate the discontinuities clinically observed in MPD and other dissociative phenomena.

As the number of these patients has increased in clinical practice, it has not been surprising to find a small body of literature that links eating disorders to dissociative states and multiplicity (Chandarana & Malla, 1989; Sands, 1991; Torem, 1986; Torem & Curdue, 1988). These contributions suggest that dissociative states often underlie a covert or overt eating disorder, but this contemporary position is actually a rediscovery of Janet (1907). This pioneer in understanding dissociative states linked the phenomena of eating disorders and dissociation together, viewing them as fixed ideas (*idées fixes*) that are concealed but treatable with hypnosis.

Acknowledging the early role of trauma and deprivation in the lives of these patients, Torem and Curdue (1988) and Chandarana and Malla (1989) urged clinicians who deal with eating disorder patients to be aware of a small subgroup of patients who often have underlying multiplicity that goes undiagnosed and untreated. Sands (1991) further suggested that eating rituals and dissociative phenomena are two sides of the same coin, a form of emotional currency used to promote survival of the self even as the manifest symptomatology is quite self-destructive. In essence, when dissociation and eating disorders occur together, they can be understood clinically as ways that a fractured self (Zerbe, 1992, 1993) attempts to deal with a variety of painful affects, experiences, memories, and even fantasies—often without symbolic, verbal modes of expression.

These recent reports are likely to be the beginning of a growing understanding in this complex area. As late as 1988, one monograph devoted solely to diagnostic issues of eating disorder patients made only one brief mention of the phenomena of dissociation in these patients (Swift & Wonderlich, 1988). The authors stressed the suggestibility factor inherent in both eating disorder and dissociative patients, likening them to the hysterical patients of earlier years. The synchronicity of symptom overlap is likewise hinted at by Hoch and Polatin (1949), who recognized the broad range of impulse disorders occurring in "pseudoneurotic schizophrenia" (e.g., borderline states). In contemporary nomenclature, at least some of these patients would span eating disorder and dissociative disorder diagnoses.

Given the frequency with which dissociative states and eating disorders may occur together, it behooves clinicians to keep an open eye to making both diagnoses if one or the other is found. In one sample, Torem (1990) found that 77 out of 84 dissociative patients had at least one eating disorder symptom (including binge eating, self-starvation, laxative or ipecac abuse, self-induced vomiting, or excessive exercising). Various treatments, ranging from cognitive restructuring to hypnosis and ego-state therapy, are suggested for effectively treating the conditions. The aim is first to provide symptom relief but then to work for enhanced self-esteem, improved body image, and better personality integration (Solomon, Gerrity, & Muff, 1992; Torem, 1987, 1991; Vanderlinden & Vandereycken, 1988).

These useful contributions serve to link two commonly observed, contemporary conditions. The more one sees dissociative phenomena as occurring on a continuum (Bernstein & Putnam, 1986), however—

perhaps even as part of the self-experience of all persons—the more one thinks of the symptoms that manifest themselves in eating disorders as bits of discontinuous phenomena themselves (Cross, 1993; Rizzuto, 1988). This perspective leads to a radical shift in how to think about and intervene with eating disorder patients. For example, no longer is self-starvation seen as a form of mere self-destructiveness or as a manifestation of the soul's longing for autonomy alone (Bruch, 1978, 1982). Rather, anorexia is understood as a hidden expression of the self, dissociated from other parts, and accessible through any number of techniques, depending on the need, potential, and talent of the patient and therapist working together. Thus some anorexic patients may gain greatest access to what motivates their self-starvation through a form of hypnosis or ego-state therapy (Torem, 1987) that addresses the self-starvation as a particular mode of self-expression (Cross, 1993; Sands, 1991; Zerbe, 1992). The therapist attempts to get the anorexic self to speak for itself, thus finding clues to the split-off or suppressed affects that have led to its existence (Rizzuto, 1988).

Although an induced hypnotic state may be a useful technique for some individuals with eating disorders who lack access to this under-belly of personal experience, many eating disorder patients find hypnotherapy terrifying. Entering a trancelike state is tantamount to losing total control, which is anathema to their taut, rigid, psychological enclaves. Nevertheless, the same principle of acknowledging the anorexia as a dissociated self-expression can be brought to the fore with more classical psychotherapeutic techniques.

For example, one young woman began a 3-year course of self-imposed starvation and isolation. Apparently, she had found comfort for a while in her cat (which died) because she could not elicit parental approbation from any other source. The patient pasted pictures of kittens all over her room, leading the therapist to reasonably conclude that the anorexia derived from a form of pathological mourning for the cat. In this formulation, the pictures were an unconscious attempt by the patient to bring the cat back to life. Interpretations along these lines went nowhere. Still, the pictures of cats continued to pepper the wall, gaining more and more ascendancy as the patient increasingly turned her back on family and peers and chose to speak little, if at all. Intuitively, the therapist guessed that an alter personality in the form of a cat had led to the patient's mute periods. One day the therapist entered the room and found the patient sitting like a cat and grooming her arms as if she were one. Only after the therapist began to address the patient from the perspective of her "cat identity" did the treatment begin to unfold. That is to say, the patient had developed a pathologically dissociated self-state as her deceased cat. Rather than lose the cat to death, she chose to be like the cat by not speaking or eating for periods of time. When the therapist began to acknowledge that parts of the patient were trying to be like the cat (i.e., not need much, not be alive, and not be hurt by other people), the patient began to brighten. In this case, the split-off, dissociated state was actually a feline alter that needed to be addressed before treatment could really begin.

In other words, just as the therapist acknowledges the reality of the patient's attempt to heal the self by forming alter personalities in MPD (Watkins, 1978), so also does the therapist acknowledge that the form of the eating disorder is an attempt to express the self, to form an identity, even to stay alive. As the five figures in *Les Demoiselles d'Avignon* may depict different perspectives and views of a woman, so might the eating disorder be conceptualized as a most personal, secretive, terrified, or childlike fragment of the individual's self-expression.

Still another common thread among multiple personality disorder, dissociative disorders, and eating disorders is that the patient may remain in treatment for years before these expressions of pathology come to the fore. As Kluft (1991a, 1991b) has demonstrated, multiple personality disorder often goes undetected and undiagnosed for years. Suddenly, alters emerge. Likewise, eating disorder patients (especially bulimic or subclinical anorexic individuals with clandestine purgative practices) keep their eating disorders out of full view of treaters (Zerbe, 1991, 1992). This deception is disheartening for many therapists who believe that they have established an excellent therapeutic alliance with the patient, only to find, several months or even years into the process, that the patient finally musters the courage to confess to late-night binges, addictive use of laxatives and emetics, and surreptitious exercise rituals. Therapists are humbled by the observations of family members and friends who all the while have fully suspected the presence of dissociative states, eating disorders, or both. Sometimes those closest to the patient have attempted to alert the professional, even conveying to treaters that there is something peculiar or incongruous about their loved one. In essence, the therapist is often the last to know.

The two disorders dovetail in yet another way. To the outside world, patients with multiple personality disorder, eating disorders, or both can lead a highly functional life (Zerbe, 1991). They are respected in their communities and make good students, mothers, and wives. One or two areas of their life may be turbulent—the aspect that is split off or dissociated from consciousness. In our sample of eating disorder patients who also carry a diagnosis of dissociative pathology, there is often one specific alter who binges and purges or starves. Imaginary companions are sought to fill inner emptiness and address the depth of despair and loneliness. Moreover, dissociative disorder patients have often been described as creative and defensive (e.g., Allen & Smith, 1993); eating disorder patients share these same qualities. Both groups of patients repeat and dramatize through their defensive style of dissociation, instead of remembering the original trauma or bringing to awareness affects that have become fragmented into the other state of consciousness.

The parallels that can be drawn between eating disorders and dissociative states give credence to seeing these states as sister phenomena occurring along a continuum. The more the therapist can address various aspects of the self—including the mature strivings for cohesion and health—the more the patient believes she can also bring the hated, demoralized, spoiling, negative aspects into full view. With these patients, therapists must always address their strengths as well as confront their acting out, because doing so furthers the patients' cohesiveness and integration (Zerbe, 1993).

Viewing the eating disorder as an attempt to preserve the self, regardless of how apparently pathological (Sands, 1991), also informs the treatment. In contrast to the less sober days of the late 1970s and early 1980s, when behavioral contingencies and strict enforcement of intake were the mainstays of most hospital-based eating disorder programs, clinicians now attempt to control the eating with less coerciveness and more insight. The life-preserving aspects of the eating disorder must be pointed out repeatedly. A trial interpretation addressing both the self-destructive and the self-healing aspects of the eating disorder might thus be: "When you stay away from food, a part of you feels alive. You feel in charge of your own life and as if someone inside is finally hearing you take control. Another part knows that you need to eat but hates to do so, because taking food in is like closing off your very breath."

It is my impression that sensitive, skilled nursing staff members have often worked in a way that addressed both the self-affirming and self-destructive aspects of eating disorders long before this kind of theoretical formulation (based on a knowledge of dissociative states, self psychology, and object relations theory) was put into place by psychodynamically informed clinicians. The nursing staff may have intuitively sensed the striving for autonomy in the face of bodily ravages that these patients conveyed by their ambivalence about eating. In any event, treaters must demonstrate again and again that the individual can feel alive in ways other than by starving or by feeling pain. The rigid superego structure forbids the total personality from experiencing legitimate pugnaciousness, lively sexuality, or desire itself (Ogden, 1989). A "suffocating self" develops, unknown (at least consciously) to other aspects of the personality, that can speak the words of anger and passion but without meaning or depth. When such powerful emotions are closed off from full expression, one outlet is the development of an eating disorder. Another may be a dissociative disorder. More often, this suffocation leads to a combination or mixture of the two, both being mechanisms to ward off affectivity.

One may see the external manifestation of starving merely by looking at the individual. The suffocating self is nonetheless split off from the patient's awareness and thus remains unknowable to the treater. A host of experiential therapies, such as art, music, yoga, and psychodrama, may be avenues for helping this secret self find expression. No matter what therapeutic routes are taken, the therapist must always be on the lookout for the reason behind the dissociation and begin to ask: Why has affect become so difficult to experience? Why did it need to go into hiding, as if placed in a large, tightly sealed urn within the person? Although patients may not respond for the longest time to such questioning techniques (which contain the seeds for rich interpretations), they will nonetheless feel heard inasmuch as the starving and suffocating selves yearn to find their own voices by an acknowledgment that they exist. The patient begins to see that looking at the fragments of her own personality is not as scary as she once thought. Her eating disorder will lose its importance as a regressive holding pattern, and she will move toward more full integration of self.

As in the painting *Les Demoiselles d'Avignon,* the patient will recognize different parts of herself, as all of us do, and have greater appreciation and understanding for those times when she knew herself less (e.g., when her eating disorder held her hostage). She may still be plagued by periods of temporary dissociation and the knowledge that there are aspects of herself that she does not know. In our experience, treatment helps the dissociative and eating disorder symptoms become less frequent, but they do not vanish for the longest time—if ever completely. The patient will come to view herself more on a journey that is exciting than one that is terrifying, leading her to yield to these defensive measures less frequently. Her world view will also be larger as her primitive yearnings will have gained expression, affect once split off will be knowable, and the parts of herself she once thought abhorrent will treat her more kindly.

This more benevolent view of a dissociated self-experience was recently conveyed by a patient in expressive psychotherapy. She remarked:

Do you remember when Mercedes came into your office and raised cain? She was the one way I could speak to all of my anger. She just tortured me. No matter what I did, she wasn't happy with my progress. She wanted to be rich, beautiful, and running the show. She's still around and happy I have a job, but I don't really notice her so much. When I get angry, I just write it down or take a long run with the dog. I don't feel like a vulture when I eat. I can even taste a steak and a milk shake sometimes.

This patient was allowing herself to let down and enjoy a host of experiences, including eating. Feelings and desire no longer had to be disavowed in a hidden "cannibalistic vulture" self. Integration, although tenuous, had begun.

References

Allen, J.G., & Smith, W.H. (1993). Diagnosing dissociative disorders. *Bulletin of the Menninger Clinic, 57,* 328-343.

Bernstein, E.M., & Putnam, F.W. (1986). Development, reliability, and validity of a dissociation scale. *Journal of Nervous and Mental Disease, 174,* 727-735.

Bruch, H. (1978). *The golden cage: The enigma of anorexia nervosa.* Cambridge, MA: Harvard University Press.

Bruch, H. (1982). Anorexia nervosa: Therapy and theory. *American Journal of Psychiatry, 139,* 1531-1538.

Chandarana, P.C., & Malla, A. (1989). Bulimia and dissociative states: A case report. *Canadian Journal of Psychiatry, 34,* 137-139.

Cross, L.W. (1993). Body and self in feminine development: Implications for eating disorders and delicate self-mutilation. *Bulletin of the Menninger Clinic, 57,* 41-68.

Davies, J.M., & Frawley, M.G. (1992). Dissociative processes and transference-countertransference paradigms in the psychoanalytically oriented treatment of adult survivors of childhood sexual abuse. *Psychoanalytic Dialogues, 2,* 5-36.

Hoch, P., & Polatin, P. (1949). Pseudoneurotic forms of schizophrenia. *Psychiatric Quarterly, 23,* 248-276.

Janet, P. (1907). *The major symptoms of hysteria: Fifteen lectures given in the medical school of Harvard University.* New York: Macmillan.

Kluft, R.P. (1987). An update on multiple personality disorder. *Hospital and Community Psychiatry, 38,* 363-373.

Kluft, R.P. (1991a). Multiple personality disorder. In A. Tasman & S.M. Goldfinger (Eds.), *American Psychiatric Press review of psychiatry* (Vol. 10, pp. 161-188). Washington, DC: American Psychiatric Press.

Kluft, R.P. (1991b). Hospital treatment of multiple personality disorder: An overview. *Psychiatric Clinics of North America, 14,* 695-719.

Kluft, R.P. (1992). Enhancing the hospital treatment of dissociative disorder patients by developing nursing expertise in the application of hypnotic techniques without formal trance induction. *American Journal of Clinical Hypnosis, 34,* 158-167.

Ogden, T.H. (1989). *The primitive edge of experience.* Northvale, NJ: Aronson.

Ogden, T.H. (1991). Consultation is often needed when treating severe dissociative disorders. *Psychodynamic Letter, 1*(10), 1-4.

Rizzuto, A.-M. (1988). Transference, language, and affect in the treatment of bulimarexia. *International Journal of Psycho-Analysis, 69,* 369-387.

Sands, S. (1991). Bulimia, dissociation, and empathy: A self-psychological view. In C.L. Johnson (Ed.), *Psychodynamic treatment of anorexia nervosa and bulimia* (pp. 34-50). New York: Guilford.

Solomon, S.D., Gerrity, E.T., & Muff, A.M. (1992). Efficacy of treatments for posttraumatic stress disorder: An empirical review. *Journal of the American Medical Association, 268,* 633-638.

Sutherland, J.D. (1993). The autonomous self. *Bulletin of the Menninger Clinic, 57,* 3-32.

Swift, W.J., & Wonderlich, S.A. (1988). Personality factors and diagnosis in eating disorders: Traits, disorders, and structures. In D.M. Garner & P.E. Garfinkel (Eds.), *Diagnostic issues in anorexia nervosa and bulimia nervosa* (pp. 112-165). New York: Brunner/Mazel.

Torem, M.S. (1986). Dissociative states presenting as an eating disorder. *American Journal of Clinical Hypnosis, 29,* 137-142.

Torem, M.S. (1987). Ego-state therapy for eating disorders. *American Journal of Clinical Hypnosis, 20,* 94-103.

Torem, M.S. (1990). Covert multiple personality underlying eating disorders. *American Journal of Psychotherapy, 44,* 357-368.

Torem, M.S. (1991). Eating disorders. In W.C. Webster & D.J. O'Grady (Eds.), *Clinical hypnosis with children* (pp. 230-257). New York: Brunner/Mazel.

Torem, M.S., & Curdue, K. (1988). PTSD presenting as an eating disorder. *Stress Medicine, 4,* 139-142.

Vanderlinden, J., & Vandereycken, W. (1988). The use of hypnotherapy in the treatment of eating disorders. *International Journal of Eating Disorders, 7,* 673-679.

Watkins, J.G. (1978). *The therapeutic self: Developing resonance—Key to effective relationships.* New York: Human Sciences Press.

Zerbe, K.J. (1991). Management of countertransference with eating disordered patients. *Psychodynamic Letter, 1*(9), 4-6.

Zerbe, K.J. (1992). Eating disorders in the 1990s: Clinical challenges and treatment implications. *Bulletin of the Menninger Clinic, 56,* 167-187.

Zerbe, K.J. (1993). *The body betrayed: Women, eating disorders, and treatment.* Washington, DC: American Psychiatric Press.

4. Diagnosing Dissociative Disorders

Jon G. Allen, PhD
William H. Smith, PhD

The increasing prevalence of dissociative disorders has spawned a range of diagnostic tools. The authors describe the use of several current methods—screening instruments, structured interviews, psychological testing, and hypnosis—and they advocate enlisting the patient as an active collaborator in the diagnostic process.

The burgeoning recognition of dissociative disorders is posing substantial clinical challenges. Experience at The Menninger Clinic is typical; we have witnessed a skyrocketing increase in diagnoses of dissociative disorders during the past several years. Not long ago, multiple personality disorder (MPD) was considered rare; now, the frequency of MPD among psychiatric inpatients is estimated to be about 5% (C.A. Ross, Anderson, Fleisher, & Norton, 1991). Yet patients with MPD are likely to be treated for several years before the diagnosis is made (Kluft, 1991a). There is good reason to hope that this latency will diminish, not only because clinicians are becoming far more alert to dissociative phenomena but also because refined diagnostic methods have proliferated.

This paper provides a brief overview of dissociative disorders and describes the range of methods that have been developed to assess them, including screening instruments, structured interviews, psychological testing, and hypnosis. We also discuss ways to enlist patients' collaboration in the diagnostic process.

Dissociative disorders

Forms of dissociation

In its prototypical form, dissociation can be construed as an emergency defense, a "shut-off mechanism" (Young, 1988, p. 35) to prevent overwhelming flooding of consciousness at the time of trauma. Yet, as Bernstein and Putnam (1986) have demonstrated, there are degrees of dissociation, "generally conceptualized as lying along a continuum from the minor dissociations of everyday life to major forms of psychopathology such as multiple personality disorder" (p. 728). Just

This article is based on a presentation at a Menninger Continuing Education conference, "Dissociative States: Multiple Personality and Other Trauma-Related Disorders," held February 14-16, 1992, at Topeka, Kansas. Dr. Allen is a senior staff psychologist in the Trauma Recovery Program at The Menninger Clinic. Dr. Smith is dean of the Karl Menninger School of Psychiatry and Mental Health Sciences at The Menninger Clinic. The authors are grateful to Judith G. Armstrong, PhD, and Eve B. Carlson, PhD, for serving as referees without benefit of anonymity.

as dissociation varies in form, it varies in adaptiveness. In the context of traumatic experience, dissociation is by definition an adaptive effort. Once learned, however, dissociation can be generalized relatively indiscriminately; at that point, dissociation undermines adaptation and becomes a disorder.

A relatively ubiquitous form of dissociation is depersonalization, a distorted experience of the self associated with a sense of unreality or strangeness and profound detachment (e.g., feeling like an outside observer, an automaton, as if in a dream). The symptom of depersonalization occurs across a wide range of psychiatric disorders, but the prevalence of depersonalization as a predominant symptom justifies its inclusion as a distinct disorder (Steinberg, 1991).

Amnesia is defined in *DSM-IV* (American Psychiatric Association [APA], 1994) as "an inability to recall important personal information, usually of a traumatic or stressful nature, that is too extensive to be explained by normal forgetfulness" (p. 478). Amnesia can be part of a constellation of dissociative symptoms (e.g., in multiple personality disorder), but it can also stand alone as a distinct dissociative disorder. In the latter case, amnesia is typically a reaction to severe stress, and the onset and termination are usually abrupt (Steinberg, 1994). Fugue could be construed as an elaboration of amnesia. *DSM-IV* criteria for fugue include sudden, unexpected travel, inability to recall one's past, and confusion about personal identity or the assumption of a new identity. Like amnesia, a fugue is ordinarily triggered by an identifiable stressor.

MPD is the most severe and conceptually challenging dissociative disorder, and a superb literature on it has rapidly developed that includes a recent book section (Spiegel, 1991), two journal issues (Loewenstein, 1991a; D.R. Ross & Loewenstein, 1992), and three comprehensive books (Kluft & Fine, 1993; Putnam, 1989; C.A. Ross, 1989). In *DSM-IV* (APA, 1994), MPD has been reconceptualized as dissociative identity disorder and is characterized by "the presence of two or more distinct identities or personality states ... that recurrently take control of behavior" (p. 484). In *DSM-IV*, amnesia also is included among the criteria. MPD or dissociative identity disorder commonly encompasses the full range of dissociative phenomena (e.g., depersonalization, amnesia) and, when present, takes diagnostic precedence.

The residual category—dissociative disorder not otherwise specified—attests to the remaining difficulty in classifying dissociative disorders. Indeed, this category may best fit the bulk of cases (Spiegel & Cardeña, 1991). For example, this large gray area reflects the fact that there are many individuals with severe dissociative experience who do not meet the criteria for multiple personality disorder (e.g., they may identify several compartmentalized and dissociated aspects of personality but may not report amnesia).

It should not be surprising that, given the recent resurgence of interest in dissociative disorders, the diagnostic classification system is in considerable flux. Davidson and Foa (1991), for example, have questioned whether posttraumatic stress disorder (PTSD) should be included among the dissociative disorders rather than the anxiety disorders and, moreover, whether etiology (e.g., in trauma) should itself become an overriding criterion in the diagnostic system. Several changes in diagnostic criteria for the full range of dissociative disorders have been instituted in *DSM-IV*, most notably the reinstatement of the amnesia criterion for the diagnosis of dissociative identity disorder (MPD), and the inclusion, in dissociative disorder not otherwise specified, of dissociation in response to coercive persuasion and trance states indigenous to particular locations and cultures (APA, 1994).

Comorbidity

Severe dissociative disorders rarely occur in isolation, largely because they develop in conjunction with trauma, and the sequelae of trauma are manifold (Kluft, 1990). As noted earlier, the overlap between dissociative symptoms and PTSD is so substantial that Davidson and Foa (1991) wondered if they should be combined diagnostically. Of course, a host of Axis I disorders may be seen in association with dissociative disorders, including anxiety disorders other than PTSD (e.g., panic and generalized anxiety) and other classes of disorders (e.g., depression, substance abuse, somatoform disorders, eating disorders, sexual dysfunction).

In addition to Axis I syndromes, personality disorders are commonly diagnosed in conjunction with dissociative disorders. Most notable among these is borderline personality disorder (BPD), and the differential diagnosis between BPD and MPD is a particular challenge. Like MPD, BPD is frequently observed in connection with a history of sexual abuse (Stone, 1990). On a descriptive level, there is a great deal of symptomatic overlap between MPD and BPD. Horevitz and Braun (1984) found that 70% of their sample of MPD patients met *DSM-III* (American Psychiatric Association, 1980) criteria for BPD. However, MPD can coexist with *all eleven* of the personality disorders listed in *DSM-III-R* and should be regarded as a trauma-induced disorder in its own right (Fink, 1991). The key diagnostic issue is the disturbance in the underlying self-structure rather than the manifest symptomatology.

Herman (1992a, 1992b) has challenged the practice of diagnosing personality disorders in patients with a history of severe trauma; she believes that this practice adds insult to injury. She construes the characterological problems as part and parcel of the reaction to severe

49

trauma, and she advocates that they be diagnosed as such. Thus she proposes the overarching category of "complex PTSD" to encompass the effects of prolonged, repeated trauma on personality and interpersonal functioning. This syndrome includes a multiplicity of symptoms, such as somatization, dissociation, and problems with affect regulation. It also involves characterological sequelae, including pathological changes in relationships stemming from traumatic bonding to the perpetrator, identity disturbance, and a proclivity to repeat the harm.

In summary, there are two diagnostic tasks: (1) Diagnose the dissociative disorder, and (2) place the dissociative symptoms in broader perspective (i.e., in relation to comorbid disorders and trauma history). Although dissociative disorders (especially MPD) have a way of capturing attention, they need not be accorded automatic diagnostic priority. A diagnosis of MPD may render comprehensible a host of previously bewildering symptoms, but a diagnosis of MPD or any other dissociative disorder should not be expected to explain all of a patient's psychopathology and problems.

Screening instruments

The most straightforward screening method is clinical observation. To foster systematic scrutiny of behavior for signs of dissociation, Armstrong, Laurenti, and Loewenstein (1991) developed the Dissociative Behaviors Checklist. This checklist consists of 30 items capturing various facets of dissociation and related symptoms (e.g., sudden changes in affect, voice, language; childlike behavior; amnesia). Although the list was developed for systematically cataloging behavior observed during psychological testing, it can also be employed for observations made during the course of other clinical interactions.

Dissociative Experiences Scale (DES)
The most efficient screening method is the self-administered questionnaire. Although a few different instruments have been developed (e.g., Riley, 1988; Sanders, McRoberts, & Tollefson, 1989), by far the most widely used and extensively researched is the Dissociative Experiences Scale developed by Eve Carlson and Frank Putnam (Bernstein & Putnam, 1986). Most patients can complete this 28-item self-report scale in about 10 minutes (Carlson, 1994). For each item, respondents make a slash along a 100-millimeter line anywhere from 0-100% (i.e., from never to continuously) indicating the extent to which they experience the symptom. The overall score is the average (from 0 to 100) across the 28 items. The content of the items ranges from commonplace experiences (e.g., driving a car and not remembering

what happened during all or part of the trip) to experiences of depersonalization (e.g., looking in a mirror and not recognizing oneself) and amnesia (e.g., finding oneself in a place and having no idea of how one got there). The response format of the DES has recently been revised to facilitate scoring (Carlson & Putnam, 1992); the DES II uses an 11-point scale (circling a percentage from 0 to 100 by 10s) instead of the visual analog scale (marking a point on the 100mm line).

In its brief history, the DES has been researched extensively. Carlson and Putnam (1992) have reviewed a host of reliability and validity studies. They report good test-retest and internal reliability, as well as an absence of differences associated with gender, race, religion, education, and income. There is, however, a low negative correlation between DES scores and age (i.e., dissociation declines with age), although there are gender differences in the pattern of age-related changes (Carlson, 1994). Considering its brevity and efficiency, the DES relates remarkably well to routine clinical diagnoses (Carlson et al., 1993) and diagnoses from structured interviews (Steinberg, Rounsaville, & Cicchetti, 1991). Patients with MPD score highest on the DES, and those with other dissociative disorders and PTSD also score relatively high. Higher levels of dissociation on the DES are also associated with a history of physical and sexual abuse (Carlson, 1994).

To screen for the presence of MPD, Carlson and colleagues (1993) recommend a cutoff score of 30, which maximizes sensitivity and specificity (i.e., correctly identifying true positives and true negatives). Because of the relatively low frequency of MPD in the population, however, only a minority of those who score 30 or above will have MPD (17% in the Carlson et al. sample). Yet a significant proportion of those high scorers who do not have MPD will have other dissociative disorders or PTSD. Steinberg and colleagues (1991), comparing the DES to diagnosis from structured interviews, found a lower cutoff score (15-20) to yield good sensitivity and specificity, whereas C.A. Ross, Joshi, and Currie (1991) used a cutoff score of 30 in their epidemiological study of MPD. Carlson and colleagues (1993) point out from their data that low cutoff scores would yield very high false positive rates. Of course, the cutoff one chooses should depend on the clinical context and the relative cost of false positives versus false negatives.

The global DES score reveals little about the nature of the patient's dissociative experience. Factor analyses of the DES have yielded clusters of items that reflect meaningful components of dissociation. C.A. Ross, Joshi, and Currie (1991) found three factors, which they labeled absorption-imaginative involvement, depersonalization-derealization, and activities of dissociated states. The absorption factor comprises relatively benign and common experiences, whereas the other two factors are likely to reflect dissociative disorders (with MPD indicated by the activities of dissociated states). Carlson (1994) reported similar factors: absorption-imaginative involvement, depersonalization-derealization, and amnestic dissociation. Carlson and Putnam (1992) pointed out that it is not necessary to use weighted factor scores to interpret the subscales; one may average the scores across items loading on each factor (see Carlson, 1994, and C.A. Ross, Joshi, & Currie, 1991, for lists of items loading on each factor). We have found a high correspondence in subscale scores between the Ross and Carlson factors, as would be expected on the basis of their substantial item overlap. Patients generally score highest on absorption, followed by depersonalization, and then amnesia/activities of dissociated states. Of course, it is not necessary to compute scores to interpret results according to subscales; knowing which factor each item loads on enables the examiner to analyze item scores according to these three dimensions of dissociation.

Use of the DES in clinical practice

From the outset, Carlson and Putnam have insisted that the DES be considered a screening instrument, not a diagnostic method. The DES indicates when to look further. In our experience, the DES can be an excellent entrée into the diagnostic process. Many patients referred to us for diagnostic consultation or specialty treatment are at least vaguely familiar with the concept of dissociation; some are highly knowledgeable about it. In such cases, the scale can be introduced as a way of helping patients think about the possible range and extent of their dissociative experience. If a patient has no knowledge about dissociation *per se,* the scale can be introduced as a questionnaire pertaining to experiences the patient may or may not have had, and an exploration of specific responses can begin paving the way for shared diagnostic understanding. Ideally, the DES can be completed and scored in advance of a diagnostic interview; if not, the patient can complete it during the interview, and the examiner can review the results with the patient immediately by scanning the items.

As Carlson and Putnam (1992) stated, the DES can be the basis of a diagnostic interview. The interviewer can go through the items with the patient, inquiring about items with high scores. For those patients whose scores are extremely low (e.g., mostly zeros), it will make sense to ask about any hint of dissociative experience. For the most pathognomonic items (e.g., pertaining to MPD), it is important to inquire about any nonzero score. Some patients, perhaps reflecting a "response bias" or defensiveness, may score very low, and even a minimally positive score may be a tip-off to significant dissociative experience. For those patients with extremely high scores across most items, the examiner may ask selectively about various facets of dissociative experience rather than inquiring about every item.

Like any instrument, the DES yields false positives and false negatives. Common among the false positives in our experience are patients with borderline disorders who experience considerable identity confusion and whose inner experience is relatively chaotic, fragmented, and discontinuous. Of course, like patients with any other diagnosis, these patients may also have genuine dissociative experience, but the dissociation may be of lesser clinical import.

False negatives are the low scorers who indeed have significant dissociative disorders. As noted before, inquiry in an interview about low (but nonzero) scores may turn up significant dissociative experiences; the low score may be the tip of the iceberg. More commonly, however, a low score may reflect denial of dissociative experiences (which can persist in the interview), lack of awareness of dissociative experience, or the fact that the dissociative experience is not active at the time of the assessment. Kluft (1991b) has noted the importance of "windows of diagnosability" (p. 168) associated with the waxing and waning course of dissociative symptoms. Accordingly, one should be cautious about ruling out a dissociative disorder. One of us had the humbling experience of evaluating a patient and concluding that dissociation was not prominent; 3 weeks later, the other author saw the patient and made a well-justified diagnosis of MPD.

Structured interviews

As described earlier, the DES can be used as a springboard and format for a structured interview that serves to clarify the nature as well as the extent of dissociative experience. A number of structured interview formats have been developed specifically for the diagnosis of dissociative disorders.

C.A. Ross et al. (1989) published the 131-item Dissociative Disorders Interview Schedule. Although it focuses on dissociation, the interview also assesses a host of related aspects of symptoms and history (e.g., somatic complaints, substance abuse, depression, Schneiderian first-rank symptoms, childhood abuse, BPD). The interview can be completed in 30-45 minutes, and it requires no specific training.

Loewenstein (1991b) has published a semistructured clinical interview, the Clinical Mental Status Examination for Complex

Dissociative Symptoms. He provided 102 items conceptualized in six symptom clusters: process (e.g., switching), amnesia, auto-hypnotic, PTSD, somatoform, and affective. In addition to presenting the interview schedule, Loewenstein included ample clinical material and guidance for interviewing patients with dissociative disorders that should be useful to clinicians conducting diagnostic evaluations in any form.

Steinberg developed the Structured Clinical Interview for *DSM-III-R* Dissociative Disorders (SCID-D) specifically to yield *DSM-III-R* diagnoses (Steinberg, Rounsaville, & Cicchetti, 1990). The SCID-D is the most refined method for assessing dissociation, and it has recently been revised to be compatible with *DSM-IV* criteria for dissociative disorders (Steinberg, 1993). The SCID-D for *DSM-IV* consists of 158 initial questions and 100 follow-up questions to be used at the interviewer's discretion. The interview typically ranges from 30 minutes to 2 hours, depending on the extent of dissociative symptomatology. In addition to being the most systematic and standardized method for arriving at a specific diagnosis, the SCID-D yields 4-point severity ratings for each of five core symptom areas: amnesia, depersonalization, derealization, identity confusion, and identity alteration. These ratings provide a profile of dissociative experience and can be summed to provide a quantitative index of overall severity. Although the interview is highly structured, conducting and interpreting it require considerable clinical experience and judgment, as well as familiarity with dissociative symptomatology. Like the DES, the SCID-D has been researched extensively, and it has been shown to have good reliability and discriminant validity (Steinberg et al., 1990). The SCID-D also dovetails well with DES screening (Steinberg et al., 1991). A Dutch version of the interview has been employed successfully in the Netherlands (Boon & Draijer, 1991).

In evaluating dissociation, interviewers should remember that dissociative symptoms are only half the picture; traumatic experience is the other half. The Dissociative Disorders Interview Schedule (C.A. Ross et al., 1989) contains more than a dozen questions regarding physical and sexual abuse. For purposes of research on the antecedents of self-destructive behavior (van der Kolk, Perry, & Herman, 1991), Herman and van der Kolk developed the Traumatic Antecedents Questionnaire. This 100-item structured interview includes a comprehensive history and provides detailed assessment of caretakers, separations, family alcoholism, neglect, discipline, violence, and sexual abuse. Not only is this history essential to provide the context of the dissociative experience, but the history-taking process may also elicit dissociative defenses in patients who are prone to dissociation.

Psychological testing

Traditional test batteries (e.g., WAIS-R, Rorschach, TAT) played a significant role in establishing the reality of MPD by documenting substantial differences among various alters. Numerous reports detailed cognitive and affective changes accompanying switches from one state of mind or identity to another (Alpher, 1991; Bliss, 1984; Wagner & Heise, 1974), differences that were far greater than mere variations in mood or attitudes across time. In addition, test results that found predominantly obsessional rather than hysterical characteristics in host personalities (Erickson & Rapaport, 1980) aided historical progress in which MPD came to be seen as a uniquely dissociative disorder rather than as merely a manifestation of "hysteria." But traditional test batteries have not proven very helpful in identifying instances of MPD that were not already suspected. With other clinical syndromes, testing often plays a significant role in detecting important characteristics that are not revealed from history and not apparent from interviews.

The presentation of MPD varies across time and mimics many other disorders (Kluft, 1991a). Efforts to identify patterns of test responses that may reveal the underlying dissociative pathology of MPD have focused on the MMPI and the Rorschach. Coons (1986) found that MMPI records often show elevations on one of the validity scales (F), and on Scale 8 (schizophrenia). The F scale comprises rarely endorsed items. Our clinical experience in using the MMPI-2 with patients who have severe dissociative disorders is consistent with Coons's findings. "Invalid" (but nevertheless useful) profiles owing to extremely high F-scale scores are routine. These high F-scale scores are consistent with the wealth of unusual experience these patients report. The MMPI seems to be throwing up its hands, as if declaring, "I can't make any sense of this!" Scale 8 also contains items dealing with unusual experiences and difficulties in realistic thinking. Scores on any or all of the other scales may also be elevated. This pattern, however, does not discriminate MPD from borderline personality disorder or many psychotic disorders.

Efforts to spot telltale patterns on the Rorschach have also failed, despite initial optimism (Smith, 1991; Wagner, Allison, & Wagner, 1983; Wagner & Heise, 1974). Recently, however, Labott, Leavitt, Braun, and Sachs (1992) have found two types of responses to be distinctly characteristic of 16 inpatients with MPD in comparison with 16 psychiatric controls: "Splitting" responses (not polarized content but rather images of figures being torn apart, separated, dividing, being cut down the center) and dissociative responses (i.e., "viewing the world through a mist or a fog so that people and objects look unclear, blurry, or far away" [p. 151]). These promising findings bear further study, particularly because Wagner (1992) suggested that the MPD sample may have been atypical. Content suggestive of traumatic experience is also a helpful diagnostic lead, because MPD is understood as growing out of trauma. Thus patients who report such percepts as assault, explosion, blood, and destruction on the Rorschach may raise the suspicion of MPD, even though not all trauma results in a dissociative disorder.

Of course, in administering any test in the battery, a sensitive examiner may note subtle shifts during the testing that indicate a dissociative process: changes in voice, posture, facial expression, handedness, mood, or approach to the task. Indeed, sometimes blatant switching occurs and the examiner may suddenly be confronted with a personality who is no longer cooperative or who has no memory of the test instructions. For example, one of us had the jarring experience of a patient entering a trance and switching in response to the Digit Span subtest of the WAIS-R (i.e., listening to a series of numbers presented in a monotone). In the absence of such switching phenomena, traditional testing approaches are admittedly limited in identifying MPD when the patient cannot or will not disclose it.

A different sort of contribution to diagnostic understanding of MPD has been made by Armstrong (1991, 1992; Armstrong & Loewenstein, 1990). She (1992) noted that, apart from either detecting or substantiating the presence of MPD, the examiner needs to understand "the deeper structure of MPD, i.e., the function of these [distinctive alter] states in the dissociated self-system" (p. 2). She (1992) has developed a testing protocol that "provides a context that encourages both the psychologist and the patient to examine the behavior of the variety of self-states within the larger self-system" (p. 2). During a pretest interview, the patient suspected of having a dissociative disorder is encouraged to express any dividedness and hidden self-experience during the testing. The interviewer comments that people sometimes feel that they have different sides to themselves, different aspects or moods. If this is true of the patient, he or she is asked to describe these experiences. This terminology is then used to guide subsequent discussion. The patient is invited to express all the self-aspects during the testing. After each test, the patient is asked how he or she approached the test and whether any problems were encountered. During the testing, the examiner may also use the checklist of dissociative behaviors to note changes in behavior or demeanor that could be products of dissociation and when they occur during the testing. This approach allows an identification of the conditions that trigger switching and traumatic reactions, so that the nature and extent of inter-alter amnesia and sharing of experience can be determined and the patient's adaptive strengths and vulnerabilities can be assessed. This creative and promising development deserves careful attention as we continue to explore the usefulness of psychological tests, not only to guide diagnostic and treatment efforts but also to gain insight into the nature of this complex syndrome.

Clinical example

One of us employed a variant of Armstrong's method to evaluate a patient with a severe learning disability. The patient had undergone psychological testing soon after her admission to the hospital and, consistent with her history of severe dyslexia, she was found to have extraordinary difficulty with a symbol-copying task (the Digit Symbol subtest of the WAIS-R). She not only copied the symbols very slowly, but she also showed mirror writing, reversing almost every symbol 180 degrees. She correctly copied only about 10% of the symbols completed by the average subject. During this patient's subsequent hospital treatment, MPD emerged. As the patient developed some understanding of herself and her alters, she was gradually able to benefit from one alter's relatively good reading skills. As part of discharge planning, the patient was retested toward the end of her hospitalization and, with other tests, the symbol-copying test was readministered.

The patient's host personality, Alice, was invited to employ the alter whom she thought would best be able to perform the symbol-copying test. She suggested that Betty might do well. Betty began the task and initially did not reverse any symbols. Betty soon began having difficulty, however, including mirror writing, and spontaneously switched back to Alice, who also had great difficulty as before. In a subsequent testing session, other alters attempted the task. The alter Catherine thought that she would be able to do the task without difficulty. She performed somewhat better than Alice, but she did the task left-handed (contrary to the other alters), was relatively slow, and reversed many symbols. Betty was invited to attempt the task again but to remain in executive control for the duration of the task rather than switching back to Alice as she had before. Betty did so, but performed quite poorly. Then Darlene was invited to do the task, because she was the alter whom Alice described as being able to write best and who was "best in school." Darlene's performance was remarkably better; she reversed only one symbol (which she quickly corrected), and she performed in the average range on the task. This dramatic jump in performance did not appear attributable to practice. Alice was chagrined by the difference, and particularly by the fact that a "younger" alter, Darlene, outperformed her. As this was discussed, however, the patient came to understand that Darlene had overcome the dyslexia by

means of grueling tutoring—itself a traumatic experience that precipitated dissociation and the formation of an alter. This discovery helped
to foster the patient's growing awareness that integration (i.e., adaptive
use of Darlene's hard-won ability) could be to her benefit.

Hypnosis

Direct contact with an alter personality is the only definitive way of
confirming a diagnosis of MPD. As a sort of controlled dissociation
itself, hypnosis can influence the dissociative barriers and allow alters
to "come out." In many MPD cases, hypnosis is unnecessary; alters will
emerge if simply asked. But if time is short and diagnostic ambiguity
persists, hypnosis can be an invaluable tool. Patients with dissociative
disorders are invariably highly hypnotizable, relying as they do on
defensive strategies that can be thought of as similar to self-hypnosis
(Bliss, 1983). After inducing a trance state, the therapist asks the
patient "if there is another thought process, part of the mind, part,
person or force that exists in the body" (Braun, 1980, p. 213). Another
approach is to ask about disremembered behaviors—for example, "I'd
like to talk to the part (or side) that cut Mary's arm."

Hypnotic interviewing does not invariably evoke alters, even when
they exist. MPD is not ruled out by unproductive hypnotic interviewing—one or more uncooperative alters may not allow communication
to occur. But when alters are accessed, another level of diagnostic
inquiry may begin, that of "mapping the system." Each alter is
interviewed and the circumstances of its creation ascertained. The
current adaptive or destructive role each alter plays in the overall
system is also determined. This aspect of diagnosis should proceed only
after a consistent treatment frame has been established and the patient
has been taught how to use hypnotic techniques for affect modulation
and self-soothing. Exploring the traumatic origins of the alters may be
retraumatizing and must proceed gradually.

Are there other cautions to the use of hypnosis? What about the
concern that MPD might be *caused* by hypnotic interviewing? Is it
possible that a highly hypnotizable individual would "produce" a new
personality in response to a clinician's implicit or even explicit suggestion
that one exists? It is true that phenomena resembling MPD can be
produced through hypnosis. Indeed, Watkins's (1978) ego-state therapy
actually exploits the capacity many people have for experiencing different aspects or sides of themselves for therapeutic purposes. It is also true
that once a patient is in treatment, the patient's dissociative processes
that have culminated in alters may continue and produce more.

But there is no evidence that judicious interviewing, like that described earlier, can actually create the complex dissociative pathology we see in MPD (Kluft, 1982). Clinicians who lack experience with MPD should use hypnosis with caution, because highly hypnotizable people may produce phenomena resembling MPD. Care must also be taken to avoid inadvertently suggesting alterations in experience such as hallucinations or anesthesias that could persist as symptoms.

Some non-MPD patients with dissociative symptoms such as amnesia ask for hypnotic interviewing to determine whether unremembered trauma has caused their problems. Sometimes recurrent dreams or fragments of memories seem to suggest early abuse, and hypnosis is sought to bring whatever is on the edge of awareness into full consciousness. There are several important cautions to such investigation. First, the recovery of traumatic memories may be retraumatizing, and may exacerbate rather than relieve the patient's distress. Even if the patient is generally functioning at a high level and does not suffer a serious regression, the revelation may trigger anxiety, guilt, and depression. Second, what is "revealed" may not be the truth the patient is seeking. We know that hypnosis increases the ability of many people to recall more about the past, but the accuracy of such memories is suspect. Hypnotically facilitated recall is subject to the same distortions as—and maybe more than—ordinary memory. What is produced may be largely true, but it may be only partly true, and verification by other persons may be impossible. Finally, the patient is left with the dilemma of what to do with the new information. If a memory of abuse within the family is recalled, how is the person to feel now about the perpetrator? And about others who may have known but done nothing? Some patients are left wiser but sadder and wish they had never embarked on the research. But some clinical circumstances seem to require that early trauma be confronted and mastered. Such efforts are typical in the treatment of MPD, and may be needed with other patients when symptoms such as flashbacks are persistent or when problems such as depression and sexual inhibition have no discernible cause and do not yield to conventional treatment. But in all cases, the cautions outlined are relevant.

The patient as diagnostician

Pruyser (1979) described the ideal of a "diagnostic partnership" in which the patient becomes "fully engaged in self-diagnosis with the help of a particular expert" (pp. 255-256). The diagnostic methods we have described have the potential to build collaboration by involving the patient in "self-diagnosis" from the outset.

There is an irony in asking patients with dissociative disorders to engage in self-diagnosis. Their experience is often highly discontinuous—at worst, utterly chaotic. Patients with uncontrolled switching and an extraordinarily fragmented identity may indeed have great difficulty collaborating in the diagnostic enterprise. But most patients, even those impaired enough to require hospitalization, are able to collaborate well, given the opportunity. Paradoxically, the same patients whose experience is so erratic are often mental gymnasts—exceptionally bright, creative, and imaginative. They are true experts in the workings of the mind. Nevertheless, the myriad alterations of consciousness characteristic of dissociation are often difficult to articulate. Patients frequently apologize for their difficulty in communicating their experience. Although they may not feel it, most patients are quite adept at describing their mental states when they are given some support.

The diagnostic work often proceeds by bootstrapping. As patients begin to articulate their experience, clinicians can begin to educate them about various facets of dissociation. Use of the various methods devised to diagnose dissociation can be highly reassuring to patients because they immediately discover that there is some universality to their experience. Seeing the items on the DES or discussing their experience in the course of the SCID-D interview gives them a sense that their dissociative experience can be put into words and is shared by others. In a more didactic vein, the simple model proposed by Allen (1993) can be used to help patients describe the nature of their unfolding dissociative experience. That is, they can be asked about gaps, blank periods, or other discontinuities in experience, as well as about the triggers that precede them and the means by which they are terminated. As clinicians educate patients and provide them with some framework for understanding their experience, the patients begin to feel understood and become increasingly able to communicate their individual experience.

References

Allen, J.G. (1993). Dissociative processes: Theoretical underpinnings of a working model for clinician and patient. *Bulletin of the Menninger Clinic, 57,* 287-308.

Alpher, V.S. (1991). Assessment of ego functioning in multiple personality disorder. *Journal of Personality Assessment, 56,* 373-387.

American Psychiatric Association. (1980). *Diagnostic and statistical manual of mental disorders* (3rd ed.). Washington, DC: Author.

American Psychiatric Association. (1987). *Diagnostic and statistical manual of mental disorders* (3rd ed., rev.). Washington, DC: Author.

American Psychiatric Association. (1994). *Diagnostic and statistical manual of mental disorders* (4th ed.). Washington, DC: Author.

Armstrong, J.G. (1991). The psychological organization of multiple personality disordered patients as revealed in psychological testing. *Psychiatric Clinics of North America, 14,* 533-546.

Armstrong, J.G. (1992). *A method for assessing multiple personality disorder through psychological testing*. Unpublished manuscript.

Armstrong, J.G., Laurenti, M.B., & Loewenstein, R.J. (1991). *Dissociative behaviors checklist—II*. Unpublished manuscript.

Armstrong, J.G., & Loewenstein, R.J. (1990). Characteristics of patients with multiple personality and dissociative disorders on psychological testing. *Journal of Nervous and Mental Disease, 178*, 448-454.

Bernstein, E.M., & Putnam, F.W. (1986). Development, reliability, and validity of a dissociation scale. *Journal of Nervous and Mental Disease, 174*, 727-735.

Bliss, E.L. (1983). Multiple personalities, related disorders and hypnosis. *American Journal of Clinical Hypnosis, 26*, 114-123.

Bliss, E.L. (1984). A symptom profile of patients with multiple personalities, including MMPI results. *Journal of Nervous and Mental Disease, 172*, 197-202.

Boon, S., & Draijer, N. (1991). Diagnosing dissociative disorders in the Netherlands: A pilot study with the Structured Clinical Interview for *DSM-III-R* Dissociative Disorders. *American Journal of Psychiatry, 148*, 458-462.

Braun, B.G. (1980). Hypnosis for multiple personalities. In H.J. Wain (Ed.), *Clinical hypnosis in medicine* (pp. 209-217). Chicago: Year Book Medical.

Carlson, E.B. (1994). Studying the interaction between physical and psychological states with the Dissociative Experiences Scale. In D. Spiegel (Ed.), *Dissociation: Culture, mind, and body* (pp. 41-58). Washington, DC: American Psychiatric Press.

Carlson, E.B., & Putnam, F.W. (1992). *Manual for the Dissociative Experiences Scale*. Unpublished manuscript.

Carlson, E.B., Putnam, F.W., Ross, C.A., Torem, M., Coons, P., Dill, D.L., Loewenstein, R.J., & Braun, B.G. (1993). Validity of the Dissociative Experiences Scale in screening for multiple personality disorder: A multicenter study. *American Journal of Psychiatry, 150*, 1030-1036.

Coons, P.M. (1986). Treatment progress in 20 patients with multiple personality disorder. *Journal of Nervous and Mental Disease, 174*, 715-721.

Davidson, J.R.T., & Foa, E.B. (1991). Diagnostic issues in posttraumatic stress disorders: Considerations for the *DSM-IV*. *Journal of Abnormal Psychology, 100*, 346-355.

Erickson, M.H., & Rapaport, D. (1980). Findings on the nature of the personality structures in two different dual personalities by means of projective and psychometric tests. In E.L. Rossi (Ed.), *Hypnotic investigation of psychodynamic processes: The collected papers of Milton H. Erickson on hypnosis* (Vol. 3, pp. 271-291). New York: Irvington.

Fink, D. (1991). The comorbidity of multiple personality disorder and *DSM-III-R* Axis II disorders. *Psychiatric Clinics of North America, 14*, 547-565.

Herman, J.L. (1992a). Complex PTSD: A syndrome in survivors of prolonged and repeated trauma. *Journal of Traumatic Stress, 5*, 377-391.

Herman, J.L. (1992b). *Trauma and recovery*. New York: BasicBooks.

Horevitz, R.P., & Braun, B.G. (1984). Are multiple personalities borderline? An analysis of 33 cases. *Psychiatric Clinics of North America, 7*, 69-87.

Kluft, R.P. (1982). Varieties of hypnotic interventions in the treatment of multiple personality. *American Journal of Clinical Hypnosis, 24*, 230-240.

Kluft, R.P. (Ed.). (1990). *Incest-related syndromes of adult psychopathology*. Washington, DC: American Psychiatric Press.

Kluft, R.P. (1991a). Clinical presentations of multiple personality disorder. *Psychiatric Clinics of North America, 14*, 605-629.

Kluft, R.P. (1991b). Multiple personality disorder. In A. Tasman & S.M. Goldfinger (Eds.), *American Psychiatric Press review of psychiatry* (Vol. 10, pp. 161-188). Washington, DC: American Psychiatric Press.

Kluft, R.P., & Fine, C.G. (Eds.). (1993). *Clinical perspectives on multiple personality disorder.* Washington, DC: American Psychiatric Press.

Labott, S.M., Leavitt, H.F., Braun, B.G., & Sachs, R.G. (1992). Rorschach indicators of multiple personality disorder. *Perceptual and Motor Skills, 75,* 147-158.

Loewenstein, R.J. (Ed.). (1991a). Multiple personality disorder [Topical issue]. *Psychiatric Clinics of North America, 14*(3).

Loewenstein, R.J. (1991b). An office mental status examination for complex chronic dissociative symptoms and multiple personality disorder. *Psychiatric Clinics of North America, 14,* 567-604.

Pruyser, P.W. (1979). The diagnostic process: Touchstone of medicine's values. In W.R. Rogers & D. Barnard (Eds.), *Nourishing the humanistic in medicine: Interactions with the social sciences* (pp. 245-261). Pittsburgh: University of Pittsburgh Press.

Putnam, F.W. (1989). *Diagnosis and treatment of multiple personality disorder.* New York: Guilford.

Riley, K.C. (1988). Measurement of dissociation. *Journal of Nervous and Mental Disease, 176,* 449-450.

Ross, C.A. (1989). *Multiple personality disorder: Diagnosis, clinical features, and treatment.* New York: Wiley.

Ross, C.A., Anderson, G., Fleisher, W.P., & Norton, G.R. (1991). The frequency of multiple personality disorder among psychiatric inpatients. *American Journal of Psychiatry, 148,* 1717-1720.

Ross, C.A., Heber, S., Norton, G.R., Anderson, D., Anderson, G., & Barchet, P. (1989). The Dissociative Disorders Interview Schedule: A structured interview. *Dissociation, 2,* 169-189.

Ross, C.A., Joshi, S., & Currie, R. (1991). Dissociative experiences in the general population: A factor analysis. *Hospital and Community Psychiatry, 42,* 297-301.

Ross, D.R., & Loewenstein, R.J. (Eds.). (1992). Perspectives on multiple personality disorder [Topical issue]. *Psychoanalytic Inquiry, 12*(1).

Sanders, B., McRoberts, G., Tollefson, C. (1989). Childhood stress and dissociation in a college population. *Dissociation, 2,* 17-23.

Smith, W.H. (1991). Multiple personality disorder and the Rorschach. In N.R. de Traubenberg & A. Andronikof-Sanglade (Eds.), *Rorschachiana XVII: Proceedings of the XIII International Congress of Rorschach and Other Projective Techniques* (pp. 134-137). Bern, Switzerland: Verlag Hans Huber.

Spiegel, D. (Sec. Ed.). (1991). Dissociative disorders. In A. Tasman & S.M. Goldfinger (Eds.), *American Psychiatric Press review of psychiatry* (Vol. 10, pp. 143-276). Washington, DC: American Psychiatric Press.

Spiegel, D., & Cardeña, E. (1991). Disintegrated experience: The dissociative disorders revisited. *Journal of Abnormal Psychology, 100,* 366-378.

Steinberg, M. (1991). The spectrum of depersonalization: Assessment and treatment. In A. Tasman & S.M. Goldfinger (Eds.), *American Psychiatric Press review of psychiatry* (Vol. 10, pp. 223-247). Washington, DC: American Psychiatric Press.

Steinberg, M. (1993). *Interviewer's guide to the Structured Clinical Interview for DSM-IV Dissociative Disorders.* Washington, DC: American Psychiatric Press.

Steinberg, M. (1994). Systematizing dissociation: Symptomatology and diagnostic assessment. In D. Spiegel (Ed.), *Dissociation: Culture, mind, and body* (pp. 59-88). Washington, DC: American Psychiatric Press.

Steinberg, M., Rounsaville, B., & Cicchetti, D.V. (1990). The Structured Clinical Interview for *DSM-III-R* Dissociative Disorders: Preliminary report on a new diagnostic instrument. *American Journal of Psychiatry, 147,* 76-82.

Steinberg, M., Rounsaville, B., & Cicchetti, D.V. (1991). Detection of dissociative disorders in psychiatric patients by a screening instrument and a structured diagnostic interview. *American Journal of Psychiatry, 148,* 1050-1054.

Stone, M.H. (1990). Incest in the borderline patient. In R.P. Kluft (Ed.), *Incest-related syndromes of adult psychopathology* (pp. 183-204). Washington, DC: American Psychiatric Press.

van der Kolk, B.A., Perry, J.C., & Herman, J.L. (1991). Childhood origins of self-destructive behavior. *American Journal of Psychiatry, 148,* 1665-1671.

Wagner, E.E. (1992). Diagnosing MPD with two new Rorschach signs: Are the signs valid or are the MPDs atypical? *Perceptual and Motor Skills, 75,* 462.

Wagner, E.E., Allison, R.B., & Wagner, C.F. (1983). Diagnosing multiple personalities with the Rorschach: A confirmation. *Journal of Personality Assessment, 47,* 143-149.

Wagner, E.E., & Heise, M.R. (1974). A comparison of Rorschach records of three multiple personalities. *Journal of Personality Assessment, 38,* 308-331.

Watkins, J.G. (1978). *The therapeutic self: Developing resonance—Key to effective relationships.* New York: Human Sciences Press.

Young, W.C. (1988). Psychodynamics and dissociation: All that switches is not split. *Dissociation, 1*(1), 33-38.

5. Incorporating Hypnosis into the Psychotherapy of Patients with Multiple Personality Disorder

William H. Smith, PhD

Psychotherapeutic treatment of persons with multiple personality disorder frequently includes judicious use of hypnosis. The author outlines widely accepted essential features of this form of treatment: developing self-soothing techniques, "mapping" the system of alternate personalities, facilitating communication between alters and with the therapist, managing abreaction, and—when possible and appropriate—aiding the process of fusion. The author shows how dissociative processes that originally were used for sheer psychic survival can be drawn on to improve psychological health.

Multiple personality disorder (MPD) is currently defined as the existence of two or more distinct personalities or personality states that recurrently take full control of the person's behavior. Generally regarded as a product of repetitive, severe trauma in childhood, MPD is essentially an adaptive effort gone awry. Dissociative defenses eventuate in a failure of the normally integrative functions of memory, identity, and consciousness. Important elements of experience and identity are sequestered out of the mainstream of consciousness, become organized as alternate selves, and reemerge in situations reminiscent of the earlier trauma. The pathology, secondary to reliance on dissociative defenses, ranges from mild to severe, and may include depression, sleep and eating disorders, substance abuse, sexual dysfunction, self-mutilation, somatoform and conversion disorders, and widespread characterological disturbances. The clinical presentation of such individuals is highly variable, and the underlying dissociative pathology may not be easily apparent (Kluft, 1991).

Treatment of individuals with MPD may contain several dimensions, including periods of hospitalization, medication for symptom amelioration, group therapy, family therapy, and expressive therapies (art, movement, writing). But there is little disagreement about the central role of individual psychotherapy (Turkus, 1991). In the healing thera-

This article is based on a presentation at a Menninger Continuing Education conference, "Dissociative States: Multiple Personality and Other Trauma-Related Disorders," held February 14-16, 1992, at Topeka, Kansas. Dr. Smith, dean of the Karl Menninger School of Psychiatry and Mental Health Sciences, The Menninger Clinic, is a diplomate of the American Board of Clinical Psychology and of the American Board of Psychological Hypnosis.

peutic crucible of a consistent, caring, nonexploitative interpersonal relationship, the person who has resorted to dissociative defenses in the face of repeated overwhelming trauma can recover the hope, trust, and dignity that were damaged by the experience. Therapy can also restore the continuity of self-experience that the reliance on dissociation had disrupted. The growing literature on both diagnosis and treatment of MPD has muted, though not silenced, those clinicians who believe that MPD is largely an iatrogenic disorder created in highly hypnotizable individuals by gullible therapists who unwittingly encourage the fragmentation of personality elements in their patients by acting as if the different elements were actually different persons. The use of hypnosis was singled out as a prime offender, because hypnosis can in fact "create" most of the phenomena characteristic of dissociative pathology. Amnesias, positive and negative hallucinations, paralysis, distortion of memory, alteration of body experience, disturbance in time sense, and the experience of actions as involuntary can all be produced in good hypnotic subjects. Indeed, there is a good deal of similarity between hypnosis and the defensive strategies used by traumatized persons, whether such strategies are consciously employed or whether, without such conscious intention, experiences become walled off from the usual flow of memory and become attached to other unintegrated aspects of identity.

Hypnosis and dissociation are not identical phenomena. Their historical definitions and contemporary measurements are not the same, but hypnosis is increasingly thought of as a "controlled dissociation" and dissociation a form of "self-hypnosis." Thus the similarity between hypnosis and dissociation has closely connected the two, and hypnosis is a valuable tool in the treatment of dissociative disorders. What was originally evoked in the individual by traumatic experiences can be beneficially influenced in treatment by controlled hypnotic interventions. Although it is true that hypnosis can *simulate* the phenomena of MPD, there is no evidence that the profound disturbances in identity, consciousness, and memory found in MPD, and the frequently accompanying symptoms of insomnia, headache, eating disorders, substance abuse, sexual dysfunction, and pervasive relationship difficulties, can be *caused* by hypnosis (Kluft, 1982; Putnam, 1989).

In the first modern treatment plan for MPD (Allison, 1974), hypnosis played a key role. Subsequently, almost every prominent author outlining treatment strategies for MPD advocates the judicious use of hypnosis. What will follow here is a summary and outline of what is widely accepted as appropriate incorporation of hypnotic techniques into the psychotherapy of MPD. It presumes a general knowledge of the clinical manifestations of MPD, a grasp of how psychotherapy is conducted without hypnosis, and familiarity with the basics of hypnosis. Training in hypnosis is now easily available through both of the nationally recognized professional hypnosis societies: the American Society for Clinical Hypnosis, and the Society for Clinical and Experimental Hypnosis. Both organizations offer introductory, intermediate, and advanced workshops, some exclusively devoted to MPD, as well as related areas like sexual trauma, self-hypnosis training, and abreactive techniques. Other teaching centers like The Menninger Clinic and numerous medical schools also provide training in hypnosis for almost all licensed mental health professionals. Using hypnosis in the treatment of MPD requires an advanced level of skill; its use in less complicated treatment situations (e.g., phobias, pain control) should precede its use with MPD.

Persons with multiple personality disorder tend to be highly hypnotizable, presumably because of their extensive use of hypnosis-like dissociative strategies in coping with early life trauma. Indeed, many theorists assert that one of the necessary ingredients for the formation of MPD is the capacity to dissociate (Braun & Sachs, 1985; Putnam, 1985). Dissociating in the face of repetitive trauma seems to strengthen that ability and may set the stage for dissociating in response to even minor stress, because the "skill" may have been overlearned.

The clinician must bear in mind that these patients may not consider what they do to be self-hypnosis. Indeed, what is experienced may not seem volitional at all, but sudden and alarming lapses in self-control. "Spacing out" or "tuning out" is a commonly reported experience, with the person's mind seeming to go blank. These individuals may abruptly "wake up" in unfamiliar or even dangerous situations with no awareness of why or how they got there. Or they may feel like a passenger or observer in their own body, with the behavior or feelings not seeming like their own.

The suggestion that hypnosis may play a useful role in treatment may be taken—as it is by many nondissociative patients—as an opportunity for the therapist to exert malignant control over them. Maintaining control over themselves in the face of bewildering alterations in consciousness, behavior, and body experience has often become a major cause of concern for such patients. The idea of surrendering self-control, much less allowing another person to gain such control over them in light of their trauma history, may be a terrifying prospect. Obviously, a good deal of education and reassurance is needed before hypnotic interventions are begun. And this education and reassurance are best provided *after* a therapeutic relationship is formed and some amount of trust in the therapist is achieved. The patient is advised that hypnosis will be used to put him or her in *greater* control, not *less*. The therapist will be teaching some techniques that can be used between sessions, and others that will be used in sessions by plan and with the patient's consent. The patient will learn to regulate the dissociative processes that were originally used for self-protection but that have taken on a divisive and maladaptive life of their own.

And what if the patient refuses? Many successful treatments have been conducted without the formal use of hypnosis, so there is no basis for considering it indispensable. For many patients, however, it has clearly been an important aid through providing relief from anxiety and other painful and disruptive emotions; assisting communication between unintegrated parts of the total personality by whatever label they may be known (e.g., alters, selves, states); relieving amnesias and abreacting traumatic experiences; achieving a sense of self-control; revising shameful and guilty self-perceptions; and fostering the assimilation of all aspects of the self and of that person's life experiences.

How to begin

Assuming a willing patient and a trained therapist, what are the first steps in the incorporation of hypnotic techniques? Simple induction techniques are usually preferable, such as eye fixation, relaxation, pleasant guided imagery, and counting. Induction techniques that involve the inability to open one's eyes (eyelid catalepsy) or move freely (arm rigidity) should be avoided because of their compromising effect on the patient's need to retain the sense of self-control. Especially anxious patients may require lengthy induction procedures (20-40 minutes) to achieve the degree of calm and the experience of safety that eventually they will be able to produce in a matter of moments. A rapid induction technique, such as Spiegel and Spiegel's (1978) method, may subsequently be used during the treatment session and in self-hypnosis.

The patient is shown how to evoke a sense of comfort by recalling a pleasant memory or devising a pleasant fantasy. Here she or he is instructed to practice producing this state of calm and pleasure periodically during the day. In time, the pleasant experience can be evoked by replacing the formal induction procedure with a signal or cue word (e.g., thumb and forefinger touching as a sign that "I'm okay"). Thus these persons learn that distressing emotions can be calmed and even replaced with pleasant ones, and that they have more control over their experience than they had come to believe. Further, the therapist is providing tangible help in putting the patients more, not less, in control. Small successes build hopefulness, self-esteem, and a sense of mastery, all of which contribute to the development of the therapeutic alliance. It is important to remember that these patients have not truly felt in control for a very long time. Neither do they have any good reason to trust the therapist. Developing trust in one's capacity for self-control and in the nonexploitative, unselfish interest of another person is precious and will grow only slowly.

Along with the pleasant memory or fantasy that is used to calm hyperarousal, the patient is helped to create the image and experience of a "safe place," something like a secluded beach, secure room, or mountain fortress where no one can approach without the patient's permission. When agreeable to the patient, the therapist may be pictured as a presence there as well. Reliving traumatic experiences for the purpose of abreaction and mastery should not begin in the safe place, so as not to contaminate it with distress. Rather, the safe place can be a place of respite following such memory work as part of regaining calm and a sense of security. The intrusion of bad memories or fantasies during these preparatory exercises signals a need for proceeding slowly and with caution.

Once equipped with self-hypnotic skills of self-soothing and regulation of emotion, the patient may begin to recall relatively minor trauma as the first step in eventual mastery of more serious trauma. Minor trauma would be experiences like being verbally berated or other stressful events that provoked discomfort but not significant dissociation. The practice of going into and out of trance can also be an important step in gaining control over what previously was experienced as uncontrolled "switching" between various states.

As the alliance is forged and the treatment frame established, the process of "mapping the system" can begin. In the most general sense, this mapping entails eliciting the various subcomponents of the personality (commonly referred to as "alters") and determining the circumstances of their creation, their age, gender, name, and role in the overall system. It is common to find protectors, persecutors, children, and opposite genders, as well as some alters that serve as single-minded expressions of hate, sexuality, or fear. A typical pattern is for three to five sides to emerge fairly quickly, then for four or five more to make their presence known. Less common are instances of larger numbers, sometimes over a hundred, but such manifestations are typically variations on a few themes rather than significantly differentiated personality states. Kluft (1988) has suggested the label of "complex MPD" for the existence of 26 or more alters.

It may be possible to identify one side that knows all the others, making initial history-gathering easier. This side may or may not be what has been termed an "inner self helper" (Comstock, 1991), an element that may be enlisted as an ally in the treatment, just as it may serve a stabilizing and protective role in the overall system. Some approaches to mapping are conducted very concretely, with the patient being asked to place his or her name on a sheet of paper, and then to place the names or descriptions of the other sides wherever on the sheet they belong. The various interrelationships between the different sides can thus be represented by their locations on the page. Even more concrete, but less common, is using the outline of the patient's actual body silhouette on a large piece of drawing paper, with alters being identified with respect to how they may be experienced somatically. Some alters may be experienced on the left or right side of the head or body, some in the arms or legs, and others in or near various organs.

These efforts at mapping carry the risk of retraumatizing the patient, because focusing on the creation of the dissociated personality elements of necessity draws the patient toward traumatic memories. When possible, abreaction of trauma for the purpose of mastery should come about by plan, not as an inadvertent reaction to history-gathering. Establishing ideomotor signaling as part of the early hypnotic training may be a valuable aid to initial mapping (Cheek & LeCron, 1968). The patient is told that other sides can communicate by lifting various fingers in response to questioning. One of the hands is identified, and certain fingers are designated to lift, such as the index finger for yes, the little finger for no, and another when the questioning should stop. Some therapists also identify a finger for "I don't know," but others consider this unnecessary or unproductive.

Early in the mapping process, any angry or uncooperative alters must be contacted. Some basic ground rules of therapy must be agreed to, such as ensuring safety for the patient's body, curtailing antisocial behavior, agreeing to develop no more personalities, and establishing the therapist's interest in the well-being of all the different sides. Although eventual integration of the overall personality is an understandable goal of the therapist for the patient, making such a goal explicit at the outset may antagonize or frighten alters who may understandably regard fusion as death for them. It may mobilize resistances needlessly and, in fact, may never become the patient's goal. After the therapist makes an accurate diagnosis and educates the patient about the disorder, the treatment alliance can be based on the desirability of increased communication and cooperation among the various parts of the overall system, decreasing self-destructiveness and maximizing adaptive functioning.

Facilitating communication

Hypnosis can facilitate the use of ideomotor signaling, with the host personality being asked to "just wait and see what happens" or even to "take a nap" so that the alters can communicate. In time, though, the host will be urged to listen in on every tolerable communication. Switching between alters can also be facilitated, with the host allowing the other sides to emerge fully for a talk with the therapist, or by the host reporting what the others are saying to the therapist.

At times, the host will be resistant to hearing any of the communications to the therapist, remaining amnestic for what transpires during part or all of the session. And it is typical for amnesias between various alters to persist, with alter B knowing about C but not about D, and so on. We must remember that dissociative barriers were created for good reasons, and only a considerable degree of safety within the therapeutic relationship will allow them to relax. An internal bulletin board can be created on which messages can be left for the therapist or for the host personality. For example, one alter might warn of the imminent dangerous behavior of another, or a heretofore silent alter might announce its willingness to be known. This is a fantasy experience comparable in some respects to the independent journaling the patient may be invited to do each day—writing done in a self-induced state of reverie or receptivity to whatever may be written, which allows the alters to express feelings and needs.

Fraser's (1991) "dissociative table technique" may be quite valuable in promoting internal communication. Patients are asked to picture themselves at a table large enough for "everyone" to be seated around in a conference-type room. From a door on the other side of the room, all of a patient's alters who are willing to be known can enter the room, sitting where they please around the table. A special switch shines a spotlight on them one at a time, determining who talks. Or a microphone may be passed around the table. For alters who are initially unable to speak directly to the host or the therapist, an intermediary may be designated. Each alter may have a memory screen nearby, allowing for the recall and sharing of traumatic memories through visualizing them on the screen. The needs and fears of the various alters can be expressed, and compromise or resolution can occur, much like a group or family therapy process.

The goal of all such techniques is to promote communication and cooperation among the different components of the personality system. In the early stages, the therapist may temporarily be a repository of information not fully shared between the alters, but this practice has many pitfalls and should be held to a minimum. Preserving secrets and having "special deals" with some parts not known by others contradict the treatment goal of openness and undermine the therapist's stance of evenhandedness. "Locating" information in the therapist outside the patient is but another form of dissociation.

Abreaction and mastery

To achieve the overarching goal of reducing the necessity for dissociative defenses, traumatic memories held by different alters must be expressed, mastered, and assimilated into the wider personality system. One of the most valuable uses of hypnosis is facilitating a modulated recall within the context of interpersonal safety that leads to a sense of mastery. Numerous articles have been published recently about the management of abreaction with hypnotic techniques (Horevitz, 1993; Putnam, 1989). The rudiments can be outlined as follows: After securing agreement from all the parts that it is all right to proceed, the therapist can use age-regression techniques that allow the memory to begin just before the traumatic aspect. Such age regression may include turning back pages on a calendar of the person's life, looking through old photograph albums, browsing in a library of old books about the person's life, or selecting from a videotape collection of all special life occasions. Watkins's (1971) affect bridge technique is often effective, enabling the patient to reexperience some recent instance of the particular emotion and to follow it back to earlier instances. Once the patient is poised at that fateful moment, the memory is allowed to proceed slowly. The goal is for the person to reexperience the event at a level of emotional arousal that is sufficient to be meaningful but not retraumatizing.

Pacing the recall is of crucial importance. Various distancing or "fractionating" techniques may be applied, such as first having the patient view the event as if it happened to someone else or to someone similar to the patient. The recall may be done in slow motion or watched as a film on a TV screen with the remote control switch firmly in the patient's hand to slow down or stop the action. What had been an overwhelming feeling can now be experienced for only a few moments, or in highly muted form. Different alters can take turns seeing or experiencing the event, slowly absorbing its reality into the life of the entire system.

Stronger and more mature alters should be expected to master trauma before the younger and less stable ones. The patient will have been trained to communicate if any alter becomes overwhelmed. In addition to the monitoring by the therapist of the patient's breathing, pulse, color, facial expression, and posture, some form of signal or of spontaneous awakening should be available in the event that the degree of distress is not apparent to the therapist. The patient should always be advised to remember only as much as can be tolerated (permissive amnesia). Provision may be necessary for the patient's physical safety during abreaction, because flailing of arms and legs is not uncommon.

The presence of a cotherapist or trusted companion is sometimes helpful. If significant violence or psychotic disorganization is a likelihood, proceeding in a hospital setting is obviously indicated.

During the abreaction, the therapist may comment about the experience, helping the patient find words to express what at the time may have been a terrifying or sickening jumble of events, although care should be taken not to guide or influence the recall in a way that might embellish or distort it. This caution is not intended to discourage the strategy of having the person take the opportunity now to tell his or her tormenter what could not have been said at the time, to express the dissociated or stifled feelings of shame, fear, or anger. The patient may even wish to punish the perpetrator in fantasy, but such a cathartic exercise is not an effort to *revise* the memory. Rather, it may help mobilize and integrate the entire range of feelings involved, and assist in countering the earlier sense of helpless passivity. The therapist can help the patient correct distorted ideas about what happened or why, so that the patient can achieve a coherent, first-person account with a tolerable degree of emotion. Mastery is achieved in part by the patient's becoming the narrator of the experience, acquiring the control that putting things into words can bring, and sharing the experience with a trusted other.

A standard 50-minute hour may not be sufficient for some abreactive sessions, but some sort of time frame should be established. Whatever the plan, Kluft's "rule of thirds" applies: The first third of the session should be spent identifying the material to be worked with, and the second and final thirds used to process the material and restabilize the patient. Some of the processing may take place while the patient is still in trance, especially in dealing with alters. Enough time should be spent with the host personality out of trance for the therapist to determine that he or she is fully alert and capable of departing safely. The integrative work following abreaction is of vital importance, because hard-won experience has shown that abreaction alone is insufficient for lasting therapeutic effect. Abreaction of every significant trauma may not be possible in those patients who have experienced prolonged cruelty over many years. The most serious traumatic events require individual attention, but others may form clusters by their similarity and be abreacted simultaneously.

Hypnosis can also be used throughout the treatment course for symptom control and management of crisis (Kluft, 1983). The patient's capacity for hypnotic responsiveness allows for what may seem like magical interventions, such as paralyzing a belligerent alter, having a frightened child alter take a prolonged nap, and temporarily creating amnesia for recent unsettling events. Such interventions should be rare. Communication between the various alters to determine the source of the crisis and to enable coping by locating and mobilizing strengths and cooperation is far preferable in the long run to coercive or manipulative control by the therapist. The ability to evoke the patient's hypnotic talents can unfortunately stir the therapist's countertransference fantasies of omnipotent control, just as it may fuel the patient's wish to submit passively to a healing caretaker. In any case, these patients are typically crisis-prone, especially with respect to self-mutilative and suicidal urges, and they sometimes require medication and periods of hospitalization despite their hypnotic abilities and other strengths.

Fusion and beyond

Integration is a gradual process occurring throughout treatment that results from the progressive reduction of dissociative boundaries, so that the individual's thoughts, feelings, and behaviors fit together coherently, providing a continuous sense of identity and ownership of experience. *Fusion,* on the other hand, refers to the occasion when selves previously experienced as separate begin to merge. They may begin to share memories, then all of conscious awareness (sometimes termed "co-consciousness") before becoming increasingly similar and ceasing to be separate. Some fusions occur spontaneously as treatment proceeds, a naturally occurring outgrowth of reduced reliance on dissociation. Others need facilitation by the therapist in the form of hypnotically orchestrated images such as of joining hands and flowing together. Fusions may be done on a trial basis, and also may spontaneously revert to separateness if done prematurely. As a rule, the therapist should not insist on promoting the fusions, because the patient's readiness is more important than that of the therapist. The alters must come to realize that they indeed will continue to exist, but as part of a functional whole rather than alone with their fear or anger.

During the period of postfusion therapy (recommended to be 2 years or so), the now-integrated alters can be elicited, either directly for face-to-face interviews or through the ideomotor signals, to determine their current degree of satisfaction and to learn of any nascent difficulties within the personality system that need attention. During the postfusion period, hypnotic techniques continue to be useful not only in affect regulation, but also in general ego strengthening, problem solving, and identity consolidation. The patient can rehearse new solutions to problems in fantasy, experiment with age progression to sample a desired new path of personal growth, and continue to draw self-esteem from the experience of mastery associated with the exercise of hypnotic abilities. The dissociative processes that were originally employed for sheer psychological survival have now become genuinely adaptive tools for the patient's developing psychological success.

References

Allison, R.B. (1974). A new treatment approach for multiple personalities. *American Journal of Clinical Hypnosis, 17*, 15-32.

Braun, B.G., & Sachs, R.G. (1985). The development of multiple personality disorder: Predisposing, precipitating, and perpetuating factors. In R.P. Kluft (Ed.), *Childhood antecedents of multiple personality* (pp. 37-64). Washington, DC: American Psychiatric Press.

Cheek, D.B., & LeCron, L.M. (1968). *Clinical hypnotherapy.* New York: Grune & Stratton.

Comstock, C.M. (1991). The inner self helper and concepts of inner guidance: Historical antecedents, its role within dissociation, and clinical utilization. *Dissociation, 4,* 165-177.

Fraser, G.A. (1991). The dissociative table technique: A strategy for working with ego states in dissociative disorders and ego-state therapy. *Dissociation, 4,* 205-213.

Horevitz, R. (1993). Hypnosis in the treatment of multiple personality disorder. In J.W. Rhue, S.J. Lynn, & I. Kirsh (Eds.), *Handbook of clinical hypnosis* (pp. 395-424). Washington, DC: American Psychological Association.

Kluft, R.P. (1982). Varieties of hypnotic interventions in the treatment of multiple personality. *American Journal of Clinical Hypnosis, 24,* 230-240.

Kluft, R.P. (1983). Hypnotherapeutic crisis intervention in multiple personality. *American Journal of Clinical Hypnosis, 26,* 73-83.

Kluft, R.P. (1988). The phenomenology and treatment of extremely complex multiple personality disorder. *Dissociation, 1*(4), 47-58.

Kluft, R.P. (1991). Clinical presentations of multiple personality disorder. *Psychiatric Clinics of North America, 14,* 605-629.

Putnam, F.W. (1985). Dissociation as a response to extreme trauma. In R.P. Kluft (Ed.), *Childhood antecedents of multiple personality* (pp. 65-97). Washington, DC: American Psychiatric Press.

Putnam, F.W. (1989). The therapeutic role of hypnosis and abreaction. In *Diagnosis and treatment of multiple personality disorder* (pp. 218-252). New York: Guilford.

Spiegel, H., & Spiegel, D. (1978). *Trance and treatment: Clinical uses of hypnosis.* New York: Basic Books.

Turkus, J.A. (1991). Psychotherapy and case management for multiple personality disorder: Synthesis for continuity of care. *Psychiatric Clinics of North America, 14,* 649-660.

Watkins, J.G. (1971). The affect bridge. *International Journal of Clinical and Experimental Hypnosis, 19,* 21-27.

6. Internal Containment in the Treatment of Patients with Dissociative Disorders

Carolyn J. Grame, MSSW, PhD

Both external and internal containment techniques are useful in treating patients with multiple personality disorder and other dissociative disorders. The author focuses on internal containment using various individualized strategies for helping these patients cope with life and work through past traumas. Because the visual imagery typically used in these strategies varies significantly from patient to patient, the author does not intend to provide an exhaustive description. The techniques are illustrated by case examples from the author's clinical practice.

Patients with multiple personality disorder (MPD) or other dissociative disorders often become overwhelmed by flashbacks, strong affects, or compulsions to repeat traumatic experience in destructive ways (Kluft, 1989, 1991; Peterson, 1992; Putnam, 1989; Ross, 1989). Such overwhelming experience can ultimately lead to chronic and severe impairment in daily functioning. Containment is therefore a vital part of treatment, so that these patients can gain mastery over their lives. According to Baker (1992), containment is the ability to experience the expression of affect without being destroyed or hurting others. Containment involves establishing strong boundaries that will not disappear easily. One such boundary separates the past from the present, so that past abuse experiences do not feel like they are occurring in the present. It may be helpful for patients to visualize drawing a white line between the past and the present to reinforce this boundary in their mind.

Much has been written about external containment for these patients (see Fine, 1991; Kluft, 1991; Putnam, 1989; Ross, 1989; Sachs & Peterson, 1992; Young, Young, & Lehl, 1991). External containment strategies include length of therapy sessions (Kluft, 1991; Putnam, 1989), boundaries on touching (Putnam, 1989; Ross, 1989), limits on telephone calls to the therapist (Kluft, 1991; Ross, 1989; Turkus, 1991), contracts on issues of harm to self and others (Putnam, 1989; Ross, 1989; Turkus 1991), and pacing of therapy (Fine, 1991; Kluft, 1989), all of which are quite important to the internalization of containment.

This article is based on a presentation at a Menninger Continuing Education conference, "Dissociative States: Multiple Personality and Other Trauma-Related Disorders," held February 14-16, 1992, at Topeka, Kansas. Dr. Grame, formerly a staff social worker at The Menninger Clinic, is in private practice in Suffern, New York.

In this paper, I will focus specifically on internal containment. Patients with MPD and other dissociative disorders are excellent candidates for the detailed visual imagery involved in internal containment methods. They have learned to use visualization extensively to survive past traumas. Specific internal containment techniques, which will be illustrated through case examples, include self-soothing through the development of a "safe place" (Kluft, 1989) and recall of good memories; use of spiritual and religious beliefs for support; use of remote control, locked doors, and other containers for the control of flashbacks; use of the "slow leak" technique (Kluft, 1989) for control of affect; use of restraints, time-out, plexiglass structures, and electrical energy for impulse control; and use of a "rage dump" ("David Calof," 1991a) for containment of anger.

Self-soothing

Kluft (1989) described the use of *"the provision of sanctuary"* (p. 94) or safe-place technique. Safe places are inner recesses of the mind where a patient's alters may go to relax and gain strength to face difficult situations. The type of safe place is the patient's choice and is unique to that patient (Kluft, 1989). The safe place can be "locked" with a "key" to reinforce the patient's sense of security. Patients may picture mountain or beach scenes. For instance, Kate visualized a decorated bedroom, and Todd pictured a field on his farm. Carrie felt very safe in the hospital and made her room on the unit her safe place.

Sometimes counting and relaxation techniques are used to help patients access their safe places. If the word "relaxation" is too threatening, then the words "peace and calm" can be substituted, or counting numbers can be used alone. Patients can take good memories with them to the safe place, or they can invoke spiritual images such as Jehovah, Jesus, or Mary.

In the beginning phase of individual psychotherapy, I find it useful to suggest that the patient recall one or more positive memories that can be used for self-soothing. I employed this approach with Anna, a patient with a dissociative disorder. During a hypnotic trance, for example, Anna recalled childhood memories of pleasant Sunday evenings when her mother bought cakes from a man who drove a bakery truck. The patient described this man as a very respectful and kind person who believed that she would grow up to be a fine adult. When Anna became afraid near the truck, he gently took her hand and led her back to the gate in front of her house. Anna smiled broadly as she recalled specific details of these occasions—the jacket the man wore, the color of his eyes, the taste of the cakes, the details of television shows she had watched while eating the cakes, and the feeling of cleanness from baths she had taken on many of those Sunday evenings.

When Anna had difficulty going to her safe place, I told her she could ask the bakery man to hold her hand and lead her there. He could then wait for her outside the door. This suggestion worked well and she became less frightened during hypnotherapy sessions. I also told Anna she could picture the bakery man nearby and recall his support and kindness anytime. He could also be with her during abreaction work. I used Anna's description of him during each session to reinforce the use of this pleasant memory. I continually stressed that the bakery man thought of her as a good person.

Another patient, Claire, who also had trouble reaching her safe place, recalled pleasant childhood memories of visiting her grandparents on their farm. She described each grandparent in vivid detail. Her grandmother wore a flowered dress with a flour-sack apron. She also always wore hose and shoes with holes cut out for her bunions. When she was visiting, Claire especially enjoyed having her grandmother warm her clothes on the stove on cold mornings.

Claire had difficulty "walking" to and from her safe place without feeling as if her legs were flying apart; she had trouble visualizing herself as a whole person. On these occasions, she wanted to come out of the trance. As she entered the trance, I repeatedly suggested that she visualize each body part connected to the others and her mind and spirit safely contained inside her body (see Baker, 1992). I also suggested that, as she entered the trance, she imagine her grandmother and grandfather walking on either side of her as she went to her safe place. Claire used her grandmother's apron to cover her legs and comfort herself. She spent time between sessions visualizing how her grandparents helped her in the present and remembering their many expressions of love to her. I encouraged Claire to remember her ability to relate to her grandparents, and advised her that she could use this ability in current relationships.

Spiritual support

Patients with strong spiritual and religious beliefs can use them for support in the trance. While in his safe place, Joe visualized his experiences of peace, happiness, and connection to a revered priest. Marilyn pictured Christ meeting her at the beginning of the trance and holding her arm just as she held her small grandson's arm. She was reminded that her grandson was the same age as she had been when she experienced the abuse. Karen pictured Christ in her safe place providing comfort and support.

Because water is often described in the Bible as a cleansing and healing agent, Elizabeth found it helpful to picture the cleansing waters of Jehovah flowing over her in her safe place and to think of His love for her. Because of her background, she found it comforting during difficult times to think of angels helping her alters to control their destructive impulses and to increase their faith and knowledge of Jehovah. Elizabeth used her belief that Jehovah does not support suicide to help her during suicidal crises. Thus messages about love, life, and forgiveness consistent with the patient's own belief system can be used in the trance to empower the person.

Control of flashbacks

One technique used to help patients control abreactions involves the use of a television room during the trance (Putnam, 1989). There the patients use a remote control to turn on the story of their lives. This method helps give them a sense of control and provides an escape if the memories become too painful. This control can be comforting to patients because they had no control over the actual abuse. They can use the remote control to change the volume, size, and clarity of the picture, to choose the place where they want the tape to stop, and to turn the picture on and off. Sometimes patients find it helpful to take the remote control with them to turn off flashbacks. I tell them they cannot lose the remote control, just as they cannot lose the key to their safe place.

Alena thought of using the remote control technique. She used it to control flashbacks when she was in her room on the hospital unit. She simply pictured walking into the TV room and using the remote control to turn off the TV set. Marilyn needed assistance in using the remote control and pictured Christ helping her turn the TV off or on. This image was consistent with her religious beliefs.

Tom controlled his flashbacks by having his memories locked behind a number of doors. One night when he felt suicidal while in a strange town, he flagged down a police car and told the police officers how he felt. They took him to a nearby hospital emergency room where they honored his request to call me. He explained that one of his doors had come open. I suggested that he shut it and lock it and throw me the key. He reported that he felt fine after doing so. I assured the nurse it was safe to discharge him, and he went home with no more difficulty that weekend.

Catherine locked flashback memories in boxes and asked angels to guard them. A number of other patients have also confined their difficult memories in locked containers between sessions. Kluft (1989) described this device as the "time-lock technique."

Control of affect

According to Kluft (1988a, 1989), the "slow leak" and "fractionated abreaction" techniques can be used to control affect from abreactions:

The "slow leak" technique ... involves the use of suggestions to the effect that the emotions in question will be experienced and dissipated slowly over time. The "fractionated abreaction" technique ... involves deliberately interrupting abreactive events after a small amount of affect has been expressed and processing what has been recovered at great length. (Kluft, 1989, pp. 95-96)

I use these techniques with a number of patients to help them be less overwhelmed by affect. They often advise me that they need to stop at a certain point in a memory. We then may need to process that part of the memory for several sessions.

Mary Ann used the slow leak technique in a slightly different manner. If her emotions were bottled up too tightly, it was because she felt too much internal pressure between therapy sessions. She therefore pictured her feelings behind a barrier that had a small hole with a tightly woven net over it. An angel turned a lever to control the amount of affect that was allowed to slowly leak through the barrier. Mary Ann could now describe her emotional states in detail instead of making only general statements about something being "too much."

Impulse control

The use of external restraints to control violent impulses in the treatment of MPD was described by Young et al. (1991). I find the use of internal restraints for impulse control also to be quite effective. Violent impulses can be checked by having the patient imagine putting adult alters who are out of control in three-point restraints. I tell patients that this technique is more effective than external restraints, and they usually agree. I tell alters to be kind and supportive to those in restraints. Over time, more alters can gradually become supportive. Child alters can be put in padded time-out rooms that are sound-proofed, if necessary. At least one adult alter stays with the child alter in time-out to provide nurturing.

This type of intervention helps the patient gain mastery over impulsive behavior and supports the positive development of both internal relationships between alters and external relationships with other people. This technique was quite effective with Marie, who used both restraints and time-out on a regular basis. She had complex MPD (see Kluft, 1988b) and required extended inpatient treatment. With the containment of impulsive behavior, she has not been rehospitalized for more than 3 years. Another patient, Andy, had an alter who was a shadow. Because neither restraints nor time-outs could contain a shadow, Andy devised a system to control this alter in which he visualized building power plants to provide electric current to a ring of light.

Plexiglass structures can also be useful in achieving impulse control (Peterson, 1992). Brandy locked several alters in a plexiglass structure where they received instruction from angels; they could be let out when they were no longer destructive to others. Stephanie locked an alter in a plexiglass house because that alter made harassing telephone calls to a staff member in a day treatment program she attended. The angel guarding this alter threw me the key, which I pretended to lock in my desk. This alter will be released at a later date. I strongly encourage patients to exercise humane treatment of alters they have locked up somehow.

Containment of anger

A number of my patients use a specific technique that Calof called a "rage dump" ("David Calof," 1991a; see also "David Calof," 1991b, 1991c). This rage dumpster is a place where it is safe to release feelings of rage without getting hurt or hurting anyone else. Each alter can have a personal safe place inside the dumpster in which to express rage. Patients can use a hose to wash away their rage from the floor of the dumpster before they leave. Rhea used this technique to contain her anger at work one day. She went to the bathroom, dumped her rage in the rage dumpster, and returned to her office feeling quite calm.

Several patients have used this technique following abreaction. After raging, they feel spent emotionally, and so they spend time resting in their safe place before coming out of the trance. This technique allows patients to acknowledge and deal with anger without becoming overwhelmed by it.

Conclusion

The internal containment techniques I have discussed are certainly not exhaustive; many others have been reported in the literature. The important point is that therapists and patients can create methods that are highly individualized. What works with one patient may or may not be helpful with another. Sometimes the basic techniques apply, and subtle changes in the imagery make them effective.

Visual internal containment works well because patients are accustomed to using extensive visual imagery to cope with the trauma that led to their dissociative disorder. Consequently, helping them to restructure their internal visualization can facilitate adaptation in their external world. One word of caution is in order: To work effectively with these patients, the therapist must first establish a good working alliance and then help the patients incorporate images that make sense to them.

References

Baker, E. (1992). *Hypnotherapy: Strategy and technique II* [audiotape]. Topeka, KS: Menninger Video Productions.

David Calof on dissociative disorders [interview]. (1991a, August). *Journey,* pp. 1-2, 4-5, 12-13.

David Calof on dissociative disorders [interview]. (1991b, September). *Journey,* pp. 3, 6, 9.

David Calof on dissociative disorders [interview]. (1991c, October). *Journey,* pp. 3-4.

Fine, C.G. (1991). Treatment stabilization and crisis prevention: Pacing the therapy of the multiple personality disorder patient. *Psychiatric Clinics of North America, 14,* 661-675.

Kluft, R.P. (1988a). On treating the older patient with multiple personality disorder: "Race against time" or "make haste slowly"? *American Journal of Clinical Hypnosis, 30,* 257-266.

Kluft, R.P. (1988b). The phenomenology and treatment of extremely complex multiple personality disorder. *Dissociation, 1*(4), 47-58.

Kluft, R.P. (1989). Playing for time: Temporizing techniques in the treatment of multiple personality disorder. *American Journal of Clinical Hypnosis, 32,* 90-98.

Kluft, R.P. (1991). Multiple personality disorder. In A. Tasman *&* S.M. Goldfinger (Eds.), *American Psychiatric Press review of psychiatry* (Vol. 10, pp. 161-188). Washington, DC: American Psychiatric Press.

Peterson, J.A. (1992). *Hypnotic techniques recommended to facilitate the processing of memories retrieved by patients (abreaction): Part I. Introduction.* Unpublished manuscript.

Putnam, F.W. (1989). *Diagnosis and treatment of multiple personality disorder.* New York: Guilford.

Ross, C.A. (1989). *Multiple personality disorders: Diagnosis, clinical features, and treatment.* New York: Wiley.

Sachs, R.G., *&* Peterson, J.A. (1992). *Guide book for video II: Mastering traumatic memories II: Special issues.* Chicago: Cavalcade Productions.

Turkus, J.A. (1991). Psychotherapy and case management for multiple personality disorder: Synthesis for continuity of care. *Psychiatric Clinics of North America, 14,* 649-660.

Young, W.C., Young, L.J., *&* Lehl, K. (1991). Restraints in the treatment of dissociative disorders: A follow-up of twenty patients. *Dissociation, 4,* 74-78.

7. Group Psychotherapy for Persons with Multiple Personality and Dissociative Disorders

Bonnie J. Buchele, PhD

Group psychotherapy is a valuable part of the treatment of patients with multiple personality and dissociative disorders. After reviewing the sparse literature on the subject, the author describes the use of group psychotherapy with these patients alone, as well as with two types of groups in which these patients may participate: incest survivors and general group therapy patients. She concludes by emphasizing the need for expert training for therapists who conduct group psychotherapy with multiple personality and dissociative disorder patients.

The number of specialized treatment programs for persons suffering from multiple personality and dissociative disorders is increasing nationwide, concurrent with the more frequent diagnosis of these disturbances. Most of the programs make extensive use of group psychotherapy; however, the literature on group psychotherapy for patients with prominent dissociative symptomatology is sparse and represents a limited integration of theory and clinical experience.

Literature review

Ross and Gahan (1988) listed group psychotherapy as a "nonessential" treatment technique for patients with multiple personality and dissociative disorders (MPD/DD). The authors said that their personal attempts at group psychotherapy have failed, but that they know other respected clinicians who have found group therapy helpful. Caul (1984) described internal group therapy—that is, conceptualizing the aggregate of a multiple personality patient's alters and host personality as a group and then conducting group sessions with an internal self-helper as therapist. Caul warned that although group psychotherapy with a homogeneous multiple personality group membership may be somewhat helpful, achieving cohesion and clear group direction is quite difficult.

Coons and Bradley (1985) described their experience as cotherapists for a group of women suffering from multiple personality disorder. All

---

Dr. Buchele is in private practice in Kansas City, Missouri. She was formerly director of the Group Psychotherapy Service and consultant to the Trauma Recovery Program at The Menninger Clinic, Topeka, Kansas.

members were in concurrent individual psychotherapy, which the authors said was essential due to the chaos and multiple crises typical of their patients' lives. The group members gained hope and worked through their use of dissociation; they also benefited from participating vicariously as other members worked through this defense as a resistance.

Becker and Comstock (1992) reported on the use of a long-term psychoeducational component in an MPD/DD group that was an adjunct to individual psychotherapy. The group traversed a developmental process in which the primary issue was divided into three phases: (1) making a connection to the group, (2) focusing on feelings of entitlement, and (3) providing a period of resolution when feelings of sadness, pain, and loss were central. The authors underscored the importance of group psychotherapy in the treatment of MPD/DD patients.

I contend that group psychotherapy is quite helpful to most patients with multiple personality and dissociative disorders at some point during the recovery process. It is usually most effective when combined with individual psychotherapy and other treatment modalities according to the needs of the individual patient. Group processes, however, can serve quite different purposes at various stages of treatment. Whatever the purpose, all procedures require that the group therapist be an experienced clinician who is firmly grounded in the theoretical understanding of dissociation, multiplicity, and group psychotherapy.

Group psychotherapy with homogeneous MPD/DD groups

Advantages
Early in treatment, group psychotherapy is most helpful when groups of multiple personality and dissociative disorder patients are homogeneous. This type of therapy often occurs on an inpatient unit of a psychiatric hospital and is relatively brief. The processes could conceivably be conducted in outpatient settings as well. However, this early treatment stage is often chaotic and filled with crises, so the support of hospitalization is desirable.

Sitting in a room with others who dissociate is one of the most powerful ways for the multiple personality or dissociative disorder patient to begin winning the battle against the sense of isolation and alienation that accompanies these disorders. Yalom (1985) referred to this concept as "universality." At last, the dissociative experiences are speakable; the notion that "going away" was a creative response to unspeakable traumatization signals the beginning of the attenuation of the fear that has hovered in the patient's mind for years—the fear that he or she really is "crazy."

The group offers a peer context, often for the first time. The need to maintain secrecy regarding intrafamilial or ritual abuse had automatically deprived these people of age-appropriate peer groups so necessary in normal childhood development. They feared punishment from their abusers and rejection by their peers if they disclosed the abuse. Acceptance by group members provides the patients with a safe place where they can experience the group as a whole as a "good mother" (Scheidlinger, 1974) who contains the terror and provides soothing—functions that were missing when the abuse occurred. By sharing their stories, these patients validate the pain and injustice they feel. The mere act of sharing and being validated leads to a sense of feeling comforted.

In the beginning stages of treatment, the group lays the foundation for starting work on two important treatment goals: (1) accepting the multiple personality or dissociative disorder diagnosis, and (2) learning that talking helps. Often the multiple personality/dissociative disorder patient has been misdiagnosed for a long time. Once an accurate diagnosis has been made, however, the patient is often catapulted into the throes of a mighty struggle over the acceptance of the diagnosis. The presence of peers who are in various stages of accepting their disorder facilitates progress toward overcoming this impediment to treatment. Patients usually first gain an understanding of what precipitated the need for other patients to acquire various alters, then transfer that insight to themselves. Understanding generates hope as patients see older group mates improve. In object relations terms, awareness gradually dawns that abusive relationships during childhood were internalized and involved part-objects, that is, "good" and "bad" objects rigidly separated from one another. Observing the amnestic barrier between personalities in others can be the first step for the multiple personality patient toward discovering the many part-objects, as well as the barriers among them, inside the self.

Members of the group learn that talking helps, not only because it soothes but also because it illuminates cause and effect, thereby facilitating self-understanding and insight. Various alters and dissociative states were created to make psychological survival possible during the abuse. As the function of this defense becomes clearer, rationality begins to prevail and the aura of "craziness" starts to abate.

Disadvantages

Homogeneous multiple personality and dissociative disorder groups also have a number of disadvantages. Group members accept without question the presence of distinct parts of themselves as well as the amnestic barriers among them. Denial that the various parts belong to one person is often tolerated and accepted, thus reinforcing the fragmented identity that is the internal price paid for such extreme compartmentalization. Group work to eliminate a patient's amnestic barrier and to promote the patient's awareness of alters for the sake of internal harmony or integration may threaten the patient's basis for membership in the group, a painful prospect indeed. Without the presence of patients who are not dissociating or switching personalities and who can demonstrate and speak to the benefits of psychological wholeness, group members—as well as the group as a whole—can become stuck in a costly quagmire of symptom maintenance rather than working toward psychological change. The defensive function of dissociation and multiplicity can then become a group resistance.

Especially in cases of multiple personality, focus on the disorder may emphasize the view of the diagnosis as a psychological showpiece. Placement in a group created especially for these patients emphasizes the distinctive aspects of the psychopathology. Members speak to one another in the jargon attached to the disorder of multiple personality (e.g., "my child alters, my internal helper"). Thus patients can receive considerable secondary gain from having such a unique set of problems. On the other hand, homogeneous groups can challenge the MPD patient's sense of uniqueness, leading him or her to experience the group as unpleasant.

The group provides a much-needed sanctuary; reluctance to disturb this peacefulness can lead to an inability or unwillingness to address competitive issues that arise in the transferences and in the real relationships among members. They may then compete to see who can recount the most horrible history, leading to the retraumatization of those present. Members sometimes express sadism in connection with their competitive urges by using trigger words that they know will precipitate distress and dissociation in their group mates. The extreme compartmentalization within individuals, in addition to the cozy atmosphere created by the homogeneity, can make it quite difficult for the therapist to address members' sadism or competition. Concomitantly, the presence of competition or sadism can stimulate a transferential replication of the group as a "bad mother" (Ganzarain, 1989), and group members may then experience the group as unsafe and dangerous. Patients may see flight (via leaving the room), dissociation, absence, or tardiness as their only ways of regaining a sense of safety.

A brief group psychotherapy session on an inpatient unit began with an older member speaking about her increasing sense of inner harmony. The cotherapists praised the woman for her hard work. One of the newer members immediately began to recount flash-

backs she had experienced the day before. Having been in the group for more than a week, she knew something of the cult-abuse histories of several members. She repeatedly used words like "hell" and "devil." One member screamed and dashed from the room. Two more curled up in their chairs, becoming silent, and a fourth ran to a corner of the room and sat on the floor. In competing with the older patient for the attention of the cotherapists, the new patient unconsciously expressed her competitive strivings and sadistic impulses by using terminology she knew to be quite disturbing to other group members. The group thus became unsafe, a "bad mother," stimulating the need to leave—either physically or by dissociating—in various members.

Group psychotherapy in heterogeneous groups

Although much of the early phase of treatment for patients with abuse histories involves mastering the trauma by telling the stories and accepting the diagnosis, these patients also suffer from characterological problems related to the abuse. Extended group psychotherapy on an outpatient basis with other adult incest survivors or in a heterogeneous population is preferable for this portion of the work. Concurrent individual psychotherapy is also desirable.

Incest survivor group psychotherapy
Multiple personality or dissociative disorder patients are readily accepted into adult incest survivor groups (Ganzarain & Buchele, 1988; Herman, 1992), because most incest survivors have employed dissociation to some extent in coping with their abuse. Thus, although the multiple personality or dissociative disorder patient is accepted, he or she is less likely to be seen as special. Acceptance by the group members makes even further inroads against the tendency to view oneself as crazy. However, giving up the sense of specialness can sometimes be very painful and may be accompanied by fear of a loss of identity (fragmented as it may be). During the lengthy course of therapy, focus on the phenomenology of the disorder, with emphasis on its adaptive aspects, is replaced by a gradual awareness of the costliness of the defense. Patients also discover the availability of other types of defensive functioning that are more adaptive in the present, given that the abuse has ended. This awareness grows through observing how other group members cope and listening to interpretations by group members and therapists alike of the maladaptation inherent in the extensive use of dissociation. As the patients work to resolve their dissociation, group and individual energies become more available for focusing on

other incest-related psychopathologies, such as self-mutilation, acting out, and somatic symptomatology (Ganzarain & Buchele, 1988).

The group as a whole, conceptualized as similar to Winnicott's (1953/1958) "good enough" mother or as a safe place, can now serve additional functions. Working through the compelling nature of the trauma in early treatment diverts the spotlight away from the betrayal implicit in the incestuous relationship, which later causes major problems and fears in relating to other persons. In the longer term group, issues of trust and the establishment of satisfying relationships are paramount. Slow, careful work is required for group members to become aware of the pervasive sense of mistrust that is fueled by an internal world of part-objects—people, others, and self who are experienced only as all good or all bad. Working through this aspect of the abuse is tedious and painful.

Quite often patients fail to recognize how a scarcity of empathic mirroring in their early caretaking relationship precipitated their narcissistic psychopathology and vulnerability to narcissistic injury. Such a chronic lack of attunement in others seems normal to these people, further complicating their ability to connect in a satisfying way with others. As previously stated, other issues must take priority early in the group treatment, but once a cohesive unit has coalesced, group members can see that empathy beginning early in life is perhaps an experience to which all human beings are entitled, and their lack of it becomes ego-dystonic. The group as a whole can then provide an empathic connection, giving rise to the hope for increased fulfillment in relationships.

In extended group psychotherapy, as the chaos in the patient's life subsides, attention should still be devoted to the triggers for dissociative episodes or switching. This task is best accomplished when these phenomena occur within the group sessions. At such times, the therapist must assume responsibility for keeping retraumatization at a minimum by reestablishing the group as a safe place and by helping the patient return to a state of consciousness where learning and remembering the work are possible. The patient can then continue to learn more specifically about the function of the dissociation. Group members should gradually understand that each individual patient is responsible for avoiding retraumatization while working through painful issues, rather than expecting the group as a whole or the therapist to carry the burden.

As a major national holiday approached, members of an extended outpatient group for incest survivors talked about their plans and then discussed their memories of previous holidays. Susie recalled, for the first time in many years, that most of her childhood holidays had been spent in hospitals recuperating from parental beatings. As she spoke, her tone and expression changed. Another member asked, "Who is here?" Susie replied that she was Dana and had never been in the group before. A third member asked if Dana protected Susie from the pain of the physical abuse, and Dana acknowledged that she did. The therapist told Dana that she was welcome in the group but that Susie was only experiencing a memory, and that she was not alone but with group members who could help her learn new ways to cope with the painful memories. The group then turned its attention to other members. Susie later announced that she had returned but could not remember what had happened. The group described her experience and the psychological work that they had tried to help her do.

Issues of competition and sadism can be addressed effectively only when the group is experienced as a truly safe, predictable place. Although most persons abused by childhood caretakers internalize both the abusive aspects and the nurturing characteristics of their victimizers, they understandably abhor the idea of an internal abuser; they strongly resist developing a conscious awareness of this part of themselves. A patient's internal abuser is often first seen and accepted, via projective identification with other group members, in the context of a group as a whole serving fairly consistently as a good mother. Multiple personality disorder patients see and deposit sadistic, competitive parts of themselves into their peers—the internal cast of characters is externalized into the group. Patients can often hear and employ interpretations of this defense as it becomes manifest in interactions during group sessions because the group as a whole is experienced as a mother in whom the good aspects will override the bad. As patients become aware of and accept their internal abusers, the changing conditions facilitate increased internal harmony or integration.

Group psychotherapy in general heterogeneous groups

Given certain conditions, much extended group work can be accomplished in a general heterogeneous group. The group must be sufficiently mature and of such a composition that members can draw parallels between their own experience and the dissociation of the MPD/DD patient; otherwise the situation may lead to further isolation and even scapegoating of patients who are struggling with this symptomatology. The MPD/DD patient may very well add to this drama by narcissistically displaying psychopathology in a bid for special status during the struggle to repair self-esteem. In addition, the group therapists must be sufficiently familiar with dissociative phenomena to know when the patient is dissociating or switching so that the group, and eventually the particular patient, can understand the meaning and function of this behavior.

One distinct advantage of the heterogeneous outpatient group is the presence of male members. Quite often, homogeneous multiple personality and dissociative disorder groups and incest survivor groups are composed solely of women. The fact that many abusers are male may contribute to the illusion that all males are dangerous. In addition, the tendency to externalize problems onto men increases when group members are all female. Because establishing the group as a safe place is essential, allowing these perceptions to go unchallenged may be temporarily indicated. However, later in treatment, when the sense of external and internal safety is more available to the multiple personality or dissociative disorder patient, the therapeutic potential is greatly enriched when male-female interactions are available for examination within the group itself.

Training of group psychotherapists

The challenges of conducting group psychotherapy with homogeneous populations of multiple personality and dissociative disorder patients demand careful, extensive training both in the practice of group psychotherapy and in the special techniques required for treating MPD/DD patients. Expertise in group psychotherapy provides the therapist with concepts such as the "group as a whole" (Horwitz, 1986); use of this concept can greatly facilitate creating and maintaining the group as a safe place. In addition, the concept of transference provides group therapists with a rich framework for understanding individual patients within the group context so that issues can be more easily prioritized in the early phase of treatment. Transference occurs in multiple forms in groups (member to member, member to therapist, and member to group as a whole), providing a way to understand patients' yearnings, feelings of specialness, and potential for retraumatization, sadism, love, and curative power. Skill in applying these concepts is acquired only with extensive training in group psychotherapy.

In addition, therapists should know how to modify the group therapy parameters and should employ special techniques when necessary. For example, they should openly acknowledge that a particular patient needs to leave through dissociation; they should help patients ground themselves; and they should accept the need for group members to temporarily leave the room. Through such techniques, therapists can support their patients' efforts to employ defenses other than dissociation to cope with the disturbing affects stimulated by group sessions.

Dissociation frequently signals retraumatization, which should be avoided whenever possible. In addition, patients who are dissociating or switching will often have no memory of the therapeutic work when they return to a normal state of consciousness. Group therapists working with this population must therefore be well trained in detecting dissociation and switching, as well as in working supportively with these phenomena.

Marlene was a relatively silent member of the group. She would occasionally experience dissociative episodes when she "went away," shook violently, and did not respond to verbal interventions. At first, the therapist would move next to Marlene, hold her hand, and talk to her in reassuring tones, thus facilitating the conclusion of the episode. Over time, the patient progressed to the point where she could be grounded with words, and the therapist ceased using touch; group members gradually assumed this function. It eventually became clear to Marlene that she dissociated whenever she started to feel angry about group changes such as the entrance of new members, the therapist's absence, and terminations. She believed unconsciously that changes heralded acts of sexual abuse, just as they had in reality when she was growing up.

Conclusion

Group psychotherapy is a valuable modality for treating persons with multiple personality and dissociative disorders. These patients may initially use it to begin breaking the secrecy, mastering the trauma, learning that talking helps, and accepting the diagnosis in brief group work solely with other MPD/DD patients. Later, extended group psychotherapy for incest survivors or with a general heterogeneous outpatient group can provide an arena for producing further harmony or integration, diminishing resultant character pathology, and healing narcissistic wounds. The challenge presented by these patients, whatever the group's composition and task, requires a therapist well trained both in group psychotherapy and in the diagnosis and treatment of dissociative and multiple personality disorders.

References
Becker, P., & Comstock, C. (1992, October). *A retrospective look at one MPD/DD group: Recommendations for future MPD/DD groups.* Paper presented at the Ninth International Conference of the International Society for the Study of Multiple Personality and Dissociative Disorders, Chicago.

Caul, D. (1984). Group and videotape techniques for multiple personality disorder. *Psychiatric Annals, 14*, 43-50.

Coons, P.M., & Bradley, K. (1985). Group psychotherapy with multiple personality patients. *Journal of Nervous and Mental Disease, 173*, 515-521.

Ganzarain, R. (1989). The "bad mother" group. In *Object relations group psychotherapy: The group as an object, a tool, and a training base* (pp. 67-87). Madison, CT: International Universities Press.

Ganzarain, R.C., & Buchele, B.J. (1988). *Fugitives of incest: A perspective from psychoanalysis and groups.* Madison, CT: International Universities Press.

Herman, J.L. (1992). *Trauma and recovery.* New York: BasicBooks.

Horwitz, L. (1986). An integrated, group-centered approach. In I.L. Kutash & A. Wolf (Eds.), *Psychotherapist's casebook: Theory and technique in the practice of modern therapies* (pp. 353-363). San Francisco: Jossey-Bass.

Ross, C.A., & Gahan, P. (1988). Techniques in the treatment of multiple personality disorder. *American Journal of Psychotherapy, 42*, 40-52.

Scheidlinger, S. (1974). On the concept of the "mother group." *International Journal of Group Psychotherapy, 24*, 417-428.

Winnicott, D.W. (1958). Transitional objects and transitional phenomena. In *Collected papers: Through paediatrics to psycho-analysis* (pp. 229-242). New York: Basic Books. (Original work published 1953)

Yalom, I.D. (1985). *The theory and practice of group psychotherapy* (3rd ed.). New York: Basic Books.

8. Family Treatment of Spouses and Children of Patients with Multiple Personality Disorder

Sue Porter, MSW
Kay A. Kelly, MSW
Carolyn J. Grame, MSSW, PhD

Although there is a large body of literature on the individual treatment of patients with multiple personality disorder (MPD), there are few accounts of the treatment of the spouses and children of these patients. After reviewing some of the existing literature, the authors present case examples of family work with patients, spouses, and children on two inpatient units and in the partial hospitalization program at Menninger. Techniques for the beginning, middle, and later phases of family treatment are illustrated.

Accounts of the individual treatment of patients with multiple personality disorder (MPD) have increased during the past several years (Kluft, 1987, 1991, 1992; Putnam, 1989; Ross, 1989). There have been only a few reports, however, on the treatment of the spouses and children of these patients. Yet multiple personality disorder causes serious difficulties in the lives of family members of such patients. Without family treatment, individual therapy with these patients may be sabotaged, marriages may fail, and children may be at risk for abuse.

Family work is an integral part of the treatment of patients with multiple personality disorder at The Menninger Clinic. To illustrate the phases of this treatment process, we will present several case vignettes from our work in both inpatient and partial hospital settings. First of all, however, a brief review of the relevant literature is in order.

Literature review

The need for educating family members about multiple personality disorder is stressed by Kluft, Braun, and Sachs (1984) and Ross (1989). Kluft et al. (1984) recommended that the education of children about MPD be geared to their age level. The educational process can include helping family members learn to recognize dissociative behavior as it

This article is based on a presentation at a Menninger Continuing Education conference, "Dissociative States: Multiple Personality and Other Trauma-Related Disorders," held February 14-16, 1992, at Topeka, Kansas. Ms. Porter and Ms. Kelly are staff social workers at The Menninger Clinic. Dr. Grame, formerly a staff social worker at The Menninger Clinic, is in private practice in Suffern, New York.

occurs in the therapist's office (Sachs, Frischholz, & Wood, 1988).

The safety of children is a number one priority, and children should be removed from inappropriate family roles (Kluft et al., 1984). In addition, appropriate boundaries should be reinforced within the family. According to Sachs et al. (1988), the most important issue when the patient is a child is to verify that abuse by family members or others has ended. These authors recommended looking for potential dissociation in the children when the patient is a parent. They also noted that children of parents with multiple personality disorder should be helped to validate their perceptions of the parent, which can enable them to relate better to the parent. Children should also be assured that they did not cause their parent's difficulties.

With regard to marital issues, Williams (1991) stressed the need to evaluate the possible abuse history of the spouse who does not have multiple personality disorder, especially any abuse by the spouse toward the patient. Marital therapy must focus on the couple's responsibility for resolving relationship problems, not just on the multiple personality disorder (Panos, Panos, & Allred, 1990). The couple should understand how affective changes in the patient may influence behavior in the relationship. Two other important issues are handling conflicting needs among alters and dealing with child alters (Panos et al., 1990; Ross, 1989). The importance of limit-setting with hostile alters was addressed by Williams (1991). In spite of the special problems often faced by couples in which one spouse has MPD, many marital therapy issues are the same as for other couples (Ross, 1989).

Difficulty in achieving sexual intimacy is a specific issue often faced by these couples. Each spouse's needs and feelings should be validated. Panos et al. (1990) recommended the use of sensitive, nurturing touch between the couple until the patient is ready for a sexual relationship.

Integration of the patient's alters can cause disruption of the family homeostasis (Levenson & Berry, 1983). Family members need to know the consequences of integration (Sachs et al., 1988). The marital relationship must be renegotiated during the postintegration phase. Stabilization of the family system is crucial to prevent further dissociation.

With regard to therapy in general, a central goal is to prevent sabotage of the primary treatment process (Sachs et al., 1988). This goal can be facilitated if family members refrain from asking the patient to divulge information revealed in therapy sessions (Kluft et al., 1984). There should be a balance between the investment in therapy and in family relationships, because therapy is often a lengthy process (Panos et al., 1990).

In the popular literature, a number of books and articles have been written on multiple personality disorder that are suitable for spouses and children (Adams, 1990; Allen & Smith, 1991; Boat & Peterson, 1991; Cohen, Giller, & W.L., 1991; Davis, 1991; Gil, 1990). In a volume of personal accounts (Cohen et al., 1991), patients, spouses, and adult children all spoke in favor of education, support, and participation by family members in the treatment process. Allen and Smith (1991) and Gil (1990) provide readable overviews of MPD. Although the book by Davis (1991) focuses on sexual abuse, there is some specific information on MPD, a section on family issues, and a section on books and other resources. Boat and Peterson's (1991) book is designed specifically for use with young children, and the fairy tale about MPD written by Adams (1990) can be used with both children and adults. The use of these articles and books can be integrated into family work during all phases of the treatment process.

Family treatment phases

Beginning phase
When the diagnosis of MPD is suspected, information provided by family members is invaluable. The following comments illustrate the kind of information provided by family members that can help treaters confirm suspicions of a dissociative disorder or MPD:

- *I feel like I'm living with several different people.*
- *One moment everything is great, but the next thing I know she is in a state of rage.*
- *Things keep appearing in the house and no one knows where they came from.*
- *I get calls at work from my wife telling me she is lost and doesn't know how she ended up there.*
- *She tells me things and then denies she said them.*
- *She is extremely forgetful.*
- *People come up to my wife and talk like they know her, but she says she's never seen the person before.*
- *Sometimes my wife will dress and act just like our teenage daughter.*

During his first meeting with the social worker, one husband reported that the patient often spaced out when she came home from work. Just before admission, she had seemed like a child when he tried to get her out of bed one morning. This input, along with that from the patient and previous therapist, was helpful in making the diagnosis of MPD.

First meetings with patients and spouses to begin the education process about MPD can prove to be quite a challenge. For example, one patient was relieved to be told a name for her illness. This relief quickly dissipated when she told her family, who reacted with disbelief. She continued to insist that it was very important for her husband to have the opportunity to hear from her treatment team their understanding about MPD. The patient struggled to accept their explanation of her illness, which contradicted her family's understanding of it as something "weird" and "strange." One family member was certain this patient was "possessed."

Problems can occur in family meetings, as demonstrated by a patient's first meeting with staff and family members. The doctor initially directed his attention to the patient's husband. On hearing the words "your husband," the patient squirmed in her chair and stated in a clear, defiant child's voice, "He's not my husband! I'm 8 years old and too young to have a husband!" She then proceeded to grab her husband's hat from his hands and placed it on her head backwards. The husband sat in embarrassed silence, vainly trying to retrieve his hat. Requests for the adult alter to come out and participate in the meeting were unsuccessful. The patient was then reminded that child alters do not belong in meetings with adults on the unit. If she insisted on remaining out, then she must sit quietly and not interfere with the meeting. The patient remained quiet but continued to harass her husband by taking items from his pockets and refusing to return them, making it difficult for her husband to concentrate on the information being shared.

In a similar situation, a patient had requested that the social worker meet with her sister to talk to the two of them about her diagnosis of MPD. The patient began switching rapidly between several hostile alters, verbally attacking and devaluing everything the social worker said. The sister was in tears throughout most of the meeting. Any attempt by the social worker to restore structure to the meeting was sabotaged by the patient. At the conclusion of a very stressful hour, the patient was asked if she had experienced the meeting as beneficial. She said, "I think it helped let my sister know me better."

In retrospect, what happened in these two cases should not come as a surprise. Most patients with MPD go to great lengths to hide their dissociation from others. It has been a way of coping in a world the patients view as frightening and unsafe. To have these defenses exposed to family members leaves patients feeling vulnerable and embarrassed.

Such problems can be reduced by anticipating with the patients prior to family meetings what it might be like for them to share information about themselves with their family. Preparation helps patients identify their fears and concerns about family reactions. What would they like their family to know about their illness? If possible, there should be agreement about which alters can emerge during the meetings. Explaining to patients what will be shared with their family is important. A patient may need reassurance that specific information regarding the trauma will not be shared at the initial family meeting.

Family education is an ongoing process. The goal is to help patients and their families learn better ways of coping on a daily basis. The family of one patient, for instance, helped her remember where she had parked the car at the mall. The family then agreed that, if possible, they would park in the same place every time. This example demonstrates how families learn to identify stressors that might cause increased switching by the patient, and how to reduce the stress or to help ground the patient in the present. Giving patients a drink of water or reminding them where they are and that they are safe can help them to emerge from a regressed state.

Weekly family meetings were used to help one patient, her husband, and their children understand the causes of her multiple personality disorder, what the diagnosis meant, and how the family members could support the patient at home after hospitalization. Neither the patient's husband nor her two young children had difficulty believing the causes or the nature of her illness. The children told how their mother would agree to certain activities but then not remember having done so. They compared their mother's times of not seeming to be there to their father's lack of response when he was engrossed in a television program. The children were told that their mother had developed a creative way of dealing with something bad that had happened to her as a child, and they were assured that they had not caused her problems. In individual sessions, the husband shared more information about his wife's early abuse history. He was aware that she had time gaps in her early memories. Although the diagnosis was painful for him to accept, he believed that it helped explain his wife's condition.

The educational process for one patient followed a slightly different course. This woman had been hospitalized several times, but the diagnosis of MPD had never been made because she had hidden the extent of her sexual abuse and her dissociative episodes. The patient's husband did not come for family meetings until it was time for her discharge. He attended several meetings in which the extent of her sexual abuse, diagnosis of MPD, need for outpatient treatment, and prognosis were discussed. Although he was quite skeptical at first, he finally agreed that the diagnosis made sense and seemed pleased that the prognosis could be good for highly motivated patients. The patient suggested that he read several publications written for a popular audience. He later reported finding the book by Cohen et al. (1991) most helpful.

In another case, the treatment team believed that the patient's husband could benefit from a simple written explanation of multiple personality disorder detailing some specific activities the patient should avoid until she was able to establish better cooperation between her alters. While driving the car, for example, the patient frequently switched to a child alter and consequently had been involved in several automobile accidents.

Middle phase
Child-related issues. The safety of children must be a priority. In one case, a patient and her husband, who was also an abuse victim, admitted their vulnerability, especially to inflicting verbal abuse, but were adamant that they had never sexually abused their children. They expressed concern about which family members should be allowed in the bathroom together. Rules about this and other issues were later worked out with all the family members present.

In another situation, a family was cautioned about leaving the patient alone with her grandson, not because of the potential for abuse, but because the patient had a child alter who took over when the baby was there and loved to play with him. At times the patient would get up in the middle of the night and wake up the baby to play.

The potential for angry, hostile alters to abuse children should not be ignored. In our experience, most of the work with these patients and their children involves providing child development education and working on parenting skills. Because of the potential for child abuse, however, the patient and family need to understand the mental health professional's legal responsibility to report abuse to appropriate authorities. In addition, the potential for multiple personality disorder in the children of patients must not be overlooked.

MPD patients have no model for what it is like to grow up in a nonabusive home or what it is like to experience a "normal" childhood. They live in fear that they will do something harmful to their children if they must set limits or discipline them. Most MPD patients try to create for their children the perfect, happy childhood they pretended they had when they were children.

Marital issues. Concerns about intimacy and sexuality often need to be addressed. Some couples feel that they have worked out these matters quite well. For others, however, sexual relationships are a major issue. In one couple we treated, for example, there was a long history of marital difficulties, and the patient often found sex to be quite uncomfortable. She and her husband began to understand this discomfort better in light of the patient's extensive sexual abuse. The husband needed assurance that he had been her only sexual partner since their marriage, and she was able to give it to him.

The issue of personal space is also a vital one. Patients with multiple personality disorder often need to spend time by themselves to regroup when experiencing a difficult situation. One patient's husband and children agreed to give her time alone when she came home from work each day. Another patient's husband agreed to honor her space in a way he had not done in the past, once he learned how important it is for these persons to feel that their personal belongings and space are not invaded because of all the boundary violations involved in the early abuse.

Family contact. Much family work can be done by telephone. Conference calls with patients and family members or with family members only are part of treatment. The process of telephone contacts before and after home visits is invaluable in identifying family stressors that contribute to dissociation. The following case example illustrates how conference calls with a patient and her family revealed the patient's disorganization and shifts in personality related to current stressors and past events.

In a telephone conference call with her family before the home visit, the patient reported that she had received a disturbing letter from a close childhood friend. She felt that this friend was angry with her for remaining in treatment. She also felt that she was a "bad girl" who had disappointed her friend.

In telephone contact after the home visit, the patient and her family made several observations. Periodically throughout the visit, the patient was slightly disorganized, withdrawn, silent, and "affectless." The patient's mother specifically noted that the patient struggled while making a presentation at a local church. The patient explained that the friend from whom she received the letter had been very involved in a church while she was growing up. The patient had great respect for her friend, who in turn had high expectations for the patient. The patient had internalized these high expectations for herself as well. The patient believed that if she failed to meet these expectations, she not only had disappointed her friend but also was a "bad girl." The patient also revealed that her friend's father had abused her when she was an adolescent, but she had never told her friend about it. The patient felt conflict about telling her friend the reasons she remained in treatment, including the abuse, because she was afraid she would lose this important relationship.

The patient's mother noted that the patient was withdrawn and silent with relatives. In this case, the patient projected her past feelings onto relatives, believing that they also saw her as a bad girl. Differentiating between the family members of the present and the abusive relationships of the past is helpful for patients with multiple personality disorder. In this patient's case, the relationship with her idealized friend brought back the painful trauma of the abuse. On her trip home, she lost track of time for several hours. She was able to relate the loss of time to painful feelings of disappointing her friend about returning to the hospital. The patient also realized that she was angry at herself for being a patient such a long time. This anger led in turn to feelings of disappointment and guilt about being unable to tolerate these emotions. All the patient's alters had guilt feelings about their existence and purpose. Family work via telephone contact assisted this patient in associating her feelings to past and current events. The social worker also was able to relay this information to the patient's psychotherapist for further exploration.

Later phase

A referral for family and marital therapy as an adjunct to the patient's individual treatment can be an important and vital part of the patient's continued treatment following discharge. The family members are also encouraged to seek out support groups in their community that might address their particular problems. Sometimes the patient's individual therapist will agree to conduct joint sessions with the spouse. In some cases, we have encouraged patients to negotiate such arrangements. At other times, we recommend a separate family or marital process.

Discharge planning is also part of the later phase of treatment. For one patient, discharge planning included an agreement with her family that she would be given some personal time and space. Family rules were written down about respecting privacy in the bedroom and bathroom and with phone calls, mail, and journals; rules were also established about touching and wearing appropriate clothing at home. The patient had difficulty with meal planning and grocery shopping, so her husband and children agreed to do these chores. A day hospital program near the patient's home was recommended, and plans for admission were completed. Our staff also recommended that the husband seek an outpatient evaluation and possible treatment for his own abuse history. The patient agreed to return for follow-up meetings related to her alcohol abuse and to attend meetings of Alcoholics Anonymous. Both the patient and her husband followed through with these recommendations.

Integration or fusion of alters seldom occurs during short-term hospitalization; this development is more likely during the final stage of extended outpatient treatment for both the patient and the family. This final stage should extend well beyond fusion so that related family issues can be addressed and worked through.

References

Adams, A. (1990). *The silver boat.* Cincinnati, OH: Behavioral Science Center.

Allen, J.G., & Smith, W.H. (1991). I am me; who are we? *Menninger Perspective,* 22(3-4), 5-12.

Boat, B.W., & Peterson, G. (1991). *Multiple personality explained to kids.* Chapel Hill, NC: University of North Carolina.

Cohen, B.M., Giller, E., & W.L. (Eds.). (1991). *Multiple personality disorder from the inside out.* Baltimore: Sidran Press.

Davis, L. (1991). *Allies in healing: When the person you love was severely abused as a child.* New York: Harper Perennial.

Gil, E. (1990). *United we stand: A book for people with multiple personalities.* Walnut Creek, CA: Launch Press.

Kluft, R.P. (1987). An update on multiple personality disorder. *Hospital and Community Psychiatry, 38,* 363-373.

Kluft, R.P. (1991). Multiple personality disorder. In A. Tasman & S.M. Goldfinger (Eds.), *American Psychiatric Press review of psychiatry* (Vol. 10, pp. 161-188). Washington, DC: American Psychiatric Press.

Kluft, R.P. (1992). Discussion: A specialist's perspective on multiple personality disorder. *Psychoanalytic Inquiry, 12,* 139-171.

Kluft, R.P., Braun, B.G., & Sachs, R. (1984). Multiple personality, intrafamilial abuse, and family psychiatry. *International Journal of Family Psychiatry, 5,* 283-301.

Levenson, J., & Berry, S.L. (1983). Family intervention in a case of multiple personality. *Journal of Marital and Family Therapy, 9,* 73-80.

Panos, P.T., Panos, A., & Allred, G.H. (1990). The need for marriage therapy in the treatment of multiple personality disorder. *Dissociation, 3,* 10-14.

Putnam, F.W. (1989). *Diagnosis and treatment of multiple personality disorder.* New York: Guilford.

Ross, C.A. (1989). *Multiple personality disorder: Diagnosis, clinical features, and treatment.* New York: Wiley.

Sachs, R.G., Frischholz, E.J., & Wood, J.I. (1988). Marital and family therapy in the treatment of multiple personality disorder. *Journal of Marital and Family Therapy, 14,* 249-259.

Williams, M.B. (1991). Clinical work with families of MPD patients: Assessment and issues for practice. *Dissociation, 4,* 92-98.

9. Nursing Care of the Self-Mutilating Patient

Catherine M. Pawlicki, RN, MSN, CS
Carol Gaumer, RNC, BSN

Self-mutilative behavior is common among patients with multiple personality and other dissociative disorders. Nursing staff members face particular challenges in managing these patients because one act of self-mutilation can disrupt the entire inpatient milieu. The authors present an approach to nursing care that focuses on working with patients to understand and develop a specific plan to curtail the self-mutilative behavior.

Self-mutilating behavior is exhibited by patients with a variety of diagnoses, including Lesch-Nyhan syndrome, borderline personality disorder, and multiple personality disorder. The behavior can range from moderate acts, such as cutting and burning the skin, head banging, and hair pulling, to major mutilation involving enucleation and amputation of body parts (Favazza, 1989). The focus of this article is on dissociating patients who mutilate by scratching, cutting, burning, or inserting objects under the skin or in the vagina.

The management of self-mutilating patients is challenging because even one act of self-mutilation can disrupt the entire inpatient milieu. It also can elicit strong countertransference reactions in nursing staff. Drawing on our experience with self-mutilating patients who display a wide spectrum of dissociative symptoms, and in particular on our work as cotherapists of an inpatient group for self-mutilators, we suggest an approach involving interventions that emphasize: (1) collaboration with the patient, (2) education, and (3) environmental support. These interventions are based on the belief that the patient must accept responsibility for changing the self-mutilating behavior. In addition, these interventions take into consideration the timing and type of support offered the patient.

In collaboration with the patients in the therapy group we led, we have developed a rationale for self-mutilation: "Obsessive impulses to self-mutilate are used as an emotional outlet and as a method for communicating self-hate, fear, anger, frustration, and mental anguish!" The patients emphasized that the exclamation point needed to be part of this statement. This form of punctuation could be understood as a metaphor for the intensity of their experience in their intra- and interpersonal worlds.

Ms. Pawlicki is a clinical nurse specialist and Ms. Gaumer is a charge nurse in the C.F. Menninger Memorial Hospital, The Menninger Clinic, Topeka, Kansas.

In any exploration of self-mutilation, two basic points should be kept in mind. First, self-mutilation is a culturally defined phenomenon (Favazza, 1989). Although our Western culture identifies self-mutilation as a pathological behavior, other cultures view it as a demonstration of a higher moral value (e.g., the Muslim practice of self-flagellation) or as a means of family or tribal identification communicated through body scarification (e.g., in African culture). Second, the patients are much more than the sum of all their incidents of self-mutilation. This viewpoint is difficult to maintain when trying to stop or limit self-mutilation on a daily basis, especially because these patients depend on self-injurious actions to mask their inner pain and their complex identity.

Causes of self-mutilative behavior

It is beyond the scope of this paper to examine in detail all possible causes of self-mutilation. Such extreme self-destructive behavior is undoubtedly the multidetermined outcome of a complex interaction of causes. Numerous explanations have been offered, including avoidance of suicide (Menninger, 1935), response to hallucinations, expression of sexual conflict, reduction of tension, and an attempt to establish ego boundaries (Favazza, 1989; Feldman, 1988). Developmental issues such as separation-individuation and attachment failure have also been discussed as possible causative factors (Feldman, 1988; Pao, 1969; Walsh & Rosen, 1988). The literature also describes a strong relationship between trauma and self-mutilation (e.g., van der Kolk, 1987). Sebree and Popkess-Vawter (1991) provided an operational definition of self-mutilation that includes both intent to injure and the consequence of physical damage to the body.

Some researchers are beginning to examine biological factors involved in self-mutilation (Favazza, 1989; Winchel & Stanley, 1991). There has been increased interest in examining the possible role of biochemical agents. Endorphins, for example, may be released at the time of a self-injurious act, which would help to explain the pain anesthesia and euphoric feelings following the act. These endogenous opiates are suspected of contributing to the addictive characteristics of the behavior. This theory is supported by the positive response of some self-mutilators to opiate receptor blockers, such as naloxone (Winchel & Stanley, 1991), and to clonidine, a medication used to treat opiate withdrawal (van der Kolk, 1987).

The neurotransmitters dopamine and serotonin also may play a role in self-injury. A possible contributing factor is hypersensitivity at the dopamine receptor sites. Dopamine antagonists have been helpful in reducing self-injurious behavior in some mentally retarded patients (Favazza, 1989; Winchel & Stanley, 1991). Serotonin may help to explain the similarities between some self-injurious behavior and obsessive-compulsive disorder. The degree to which self-mutilative behavior is influenced by any of these biochemical imbalances is unclear.

A psychodynamic perspective

Basic to effective nursing interventions is a psychodynamic formulation of self-mutilation. Although psychiatric nurses work with relationships that patients develop in the here and now, the self-mutilator's relationship patterns have been most strongly influenced by early developmental loss (Walsh & Rosen, 1988). We speculate that persons who resort to self-mutilation to regulate affect have experienced a profound empathic failure in their relationships with caregivers. Lacking an empathic, intimate relationship, these persons have not been able to successfully communicate feelings, and have not felt genuinely understood by their caregivers. If predisposed individuals fail to form an attachment to an empathic caretaker who can contain overwhelming anxiety, they may resort to dissociation. Although dissociation may bind the anxiety, it seals off memory and affect from the traumatic event. As a result of the excessive use of dissociation, these patients experience themselves and significant others as fragmented and illusory figures. The need for attachment remains and is constantly sought after, but may be only dysfunctionally satisfied (e.g., attachment to the abuser). Personality development in the context of overwhelming anxiety and consequent coping through the excessive use of dissociation seriously impedes the acquisition of the skill of putting feelings into words. Thus, for the self-mutilator, interpersonal attachments are sought with the hope of achieving what has never been experienced—empathic attunement. For the self-mutilator, the idealized attachment almost inevitably becomes a terrorizing, disappointing experience because normal frustrations resonate with the original empathic failure.

The typical pattern we see in self-mutilating patients is that any behavior by the nursing staff that a patient perceives as a loss immediately recapitulates the patient's initial, profound developmental loss. Data collected with a flow sheet on our unit confirmed the high-risk times of perceived loss: shift change, break time for staff members, and milieu crises when acting out by other patients requires additional staff time. The self-mutilating patient experiences these common unit incidents as empathic failures by the nursing staff.

A perceived empathic failure triggers intrapsychic changes in the patient. Initially, the patient experiences what Peplau (1963) described as a "felt need" not to be abandoned, but the patient is unable to verbalize feelings about this unmet need. During this "arousal state" (Walsh & Rosen, 1988), the patient experiences mounting and increasingly intolerable tension from the unmet need. Unless this state is interrupted, the patient regresses to a preverbal condition and experiences a profound fragmentation of self and body. At this point, the patient is incapable of resisting the urge to self-mutilate. Nurses have often said to such patients, "Tell us when you feel the urge to mutilate." This is an impossible task for the patient in a preverbal state. The self-mutilative act serves to reunite self and body, to symbolically punish whomever the nurse represents, and to express self-loathing and blame. It is our hypothesis that the severity of the fragmentation the patient has experienced can be estimated by the time lapse between the act (which promotes intrapsychic organization) and the patient's communication about the act (a conscious, interpersonal phenomenon).

Nursing interventions

The primary nursing care goal with self-mutilating patients is to help them create a safe environment for themselves and assume responsibility for their behavior. We will describe the following areas of focus for nursing care: (1) modulation of attachment in the nurse-patient relationship, (2) affect regulation, (3) interruption of arousal state, (4) contracting, (5) wound care, (6) distinguishing between suicide and self-mutilation, and (7) milieu management.

Conceptualizing the nurse-patient relationship

Because of the dysfunctional attachment pattern of self-mutilating patients, we have conceptualized a model of nursing care delivery that assists patients in achieving a corrective experience in interpersonal attachment. The model emphasizes helping a patient learn to modulate attachments, and at the same time to experience a degree of consistency, predictability, wholeness, and control in a relationship.

In the model, the nurse coordinator collaborates with the patient in developing the plan of care. The nurse coordinator and the patient work in a structured format, using the nursing care plan as the focus of their work. The patient is assigned a different "shift associate" for each work shift during the day. This nursing staff member assumes the role of coach with the patient as they work together to implement the care plan. Structure in the nurse-patient relationship provides predictability and minimizes empathic failure. The involvement of numerous members of the nursing staff enables the patient to modulate attachments and assists the staff in managing countertransference.

108

This model of nursing has been formalized in a written document that delineates patient, coordinator, and shift associate responsibilities. The model is discussed with the patient during telephone contact before admission and is reviewed after the patient has been admitted. The patient is thus taught both formally and experientially how to work in the relationship.

Affect regulation

Patients often use self-mutilating behavior as a way to contain affect. Nursing care is directed at helping patients develop awareness of their feelings, and to label and manage those feelings. These interventions are *not* aimed primarily at helping them develop insight into unconscious motivation, but rather at acquiring cognitive and emotional skills that will enhance affect regulation. Experiential learning is facilitated by discussing simple everyday occurrences and labeling the accompanying feelings. Formal teaching is also needed at intervals to correct misperceptions of certain feelings.

An important area of teaching involves the use of self-soothing techniques. Patients need assistance in differentiating appropriate from inappropriate self-soothing. Education is helpful regarding the possible biochemical role of endorphins and neurotransmitters as internal reinforcers of the mutilation. Patients can be directed to use physical exercise as an outlet for tension that might otherwise cause endorphins to be released. It is also important to help these patients build a repertoire of self-soothing techniques, such as listening to a relaxation tape, taking a warm bath, or holding a teddy bear. In addition, the use of a "safe place" is helpful for patients. A safe place is a particular location in the environment or an image that can be evoked to promote a sense of safety and soothing. These patients will often look for soothing through spending time with a member of the nursing staff, which is not always beneficial. Helping patients learn how to soothe themselves is essential for a successful transition out of the hospital.

Anger is a difficult and often forbidden feeling for these patients. In childhood, many of these persons were exposed to overwhelming anger by their caretakers, which they often managed through dissociation. Physical or emotional abandonment in childhood left them with unexpressed rage. The rage was unexpressed because it was dissociated or the environment was too hostile to allow for any overt expression. Anger represented "badness," and badness demanded punishment. For these individuals, the punishment is most safely administered by self-mutilation. As patients begin to exert conscious control over self-mutilative acts, they will experience more affect, notably unmodulated anger.

Nursing care should always include a plan to help the patient develop anger management skills. The plan, worked out with the patient, may include journaling, physical activity, medication, talking, or using a safe place. It may also include voluntary restraints. That is, the patient either asks to be put in restraints or readily agrees with the staff's suggestion to be put in restraints. Nurses (and other treaters) may be concerned that the use of restraints will recapitulate past abuse experiences. When a patient requests restraints, however, our experience indicates that the patient does not want to become out of control (like the abuser) and is hopeful that the anger will not destroy others.

Interruption of the arousal state

Another important area of collaboration with patients involves the development of a specific plan to interrupt the arousal state that occurs prior to self-mutilative behavior. Patients typically will have a lack of awareness of their pattern of mutilation, feeling that the urge to mutilate comes from nowhere.

The first step in the plan involves helping patients learn to recognize their high-risk times and triggers. The patient first prioritizes four to six common early warning signs. Two common situations are: (1) an event in which a high level of affect is expressed or experienced, and (2) a time of the day when there may be less structure and increased isolation (e.g., evening hours and weekends).

The next step is to develop a specific plan of action to help the patient feel in control and maintain safety. This plan of action usually involves four aspects: (1) increasing involvement with others, (2) initiating physical activity such as vigorous walking or throwing a ball, (3) engaging in self-soothing activities that provide distraction and reduce tension (e.g., playing games, watching TV, listening to relaxation tapes, painting), and (4) processing the feelings by talking or journaling.

To be effective, this plan should be implemented before the patient reaches the preverbal state. It should be written down, carried by the patient at all times, and posted in the patient's room. Primary support people should be familiar with it. It should be periodically reviewed and updated, first in consultation with the nurse coordinator and then by the patient independently. The plan helps patients develop control over their impulses and supports the development of healthy coping skills to replace the mutilating behavior.

Individualized contracts

A question that often arises when working with these patients concerns the use of contracts. During the early phases of hospital treatment, short-term contracts (e.g., "I can be safe while taking a shower") can be quite helpful. The patient feels some success at maintaining control over impulses for the agreed-upon time. Longer term contracts (e.g., "I will not self-mutilate during the hospital stay") are usually unrealistic for the patient and reflect wishful thinking by the staff. Such a contract often stops the communication, not the behavior. Some self-mutilators will need to test such a contract. Their mutilation may be a minor episode, such as a superficial scratch, but staff members must be willing to carry out the agreed-upon consequences for breaking the contract.

Contracts can be useful in later phases of treatment when the patient has developed the skills to talk about his or her feelings. Contracts can also be a useful adjunct to outpatient therapy. In general, individualized contracts can be used as a tool to foster patients' development of impulse control.

Wound care

A desired patient outcome is the replacement of self-mutilating behavior with self-healing behavior. This development is facilitated in part by a consistent approach to wound care. Within a week of admission, each patient with a history of current self-mutilation is taught how to care for simple wounds, including appropriate wound cleansing, signs and symptoms of wound infection, and nutrition for wound healing. After a wound is inflicted, nursing staff attention should be minimized and the patient should be expected to provide self-care of the wound when medically indicated.

Suicide versus self-mutilation

An admittedly controversial premise in any discussion about self-mutilation is that it requires different interventions than suicide does because self-mutilation is not a suicide attempt. The goal of self-mutilation is to feel alive and to concretize emotional pain into physical pain. The goal of suicide, on the other hand, is to cease consciousness and to end all pain. Self-mutilators can become depressed and suicidal, or can accidentally kill themselves, but we share Walsh and Rosen's (1988) view that self-mutilation is not in itself a suicidal act.

Continual assessment is required to determine whether a self-mutilator has shifted to a more suicidal state. This assessment should be based on the potential lethality of the self-injurious plans or actions; the level of depression; the degree of disorganization; and the extent of external stressors, especially involving losses. The assessment cannot be based solely on what the patient verbalizes as the intention, because the patient may not be aware of the intent.

To emphasize the importance of understanding and responding to patients' motivation for self-mutilation (i.e., to feel alive and to relieve tension), a set of nursing interventions called "Levels of Alertness" (LOA) was created (see Table 1). There are three levels of intervention. Level I indicates the presence of warning signs for the individual, and Levels II and III are interventions for the patient who has mutilated, has inflicted serious tissue damage, or is at high risk for such behavior. Key elements of the Levels of Alertness are response to warning signs, support and documentation of anger management, and provision of a safe and containing environment.

Milieu management

Self-mutilation has a powerful impact on the milieu. It can, for example, precipitate contagion behavior among other patients. The peer relationships of self-mutilators exhibit a rescuer-victim pattern (Walsh & Rosen, 1988). This subtle pattern is difficult to distinguish from a healthy, caring relationship. Frequent reports by one patient about another who self-mutilates are dysfunctional and should be confronted as such. Other patients need to be taught the difference between positive and negative support for the self-mutilator; for example, an outpouring of affection after an act of self-mutilation actually reinforces the behavior.

Self-mutilation contagion in a milieu can be very stressful for staff and patients. Opportunities to address group issues openly help diminish competition and provide alternative communication channels (Walsh & Rosen, 1988). Secrets need to be anticipated and confronted directly.

The understanding and appropriate control of countertransference in nursing staff is a key element in effective overall milieu management. Countertransference can be manifested in many ways: avoiding the patient, labeling the patient as a "cutter," feeling like a hostage, expressing excessive sympathy about the injury, or entertaining a wish to retaliate. Helping the staff to control countertransference is a continual process. An atmosphere for appropriate ventilation of staff feelings is essential, because it allows for validation and exploration of nurse-patient dynamics.

Effective milieu management also involves using the previously described model of nursing care to help nursing staff members stay attached without becoming overwhelmed by the neediness of these patients. In addition, not blaming any staff member for a patient self-mutilation is paramount. At the same time, nursing staff members are actively encouraged to review incidents of mutilation from a learning perspective as a way to increase their understanding of patient dynamics.

Finally, the current reality of AIDS means that exposure to blood and infected wounds is a real physical and psychological issue for nursing

Table 1. *Levels of Alertness*

Activity	Level I Alertness	Level II Alertness	Level III Alertness
Degree of supervision/rounds	15-minute rounds during day and evening until sleeping for night or for period at high risk.	15-minute rounds. Lights on dim in room through the night. In direct view of staff during high-risk times per care plan.	15-minute rounds. One-on-one. Lights on dim in room throughout the night.
Closets/drawers	Items/areas commonly used by patient for self-harm are locked up.	All items/areas locked (cigarette lighter at desk).	All items/areas locked up. Any item used to harm self not to be used at all on this level.
Room search	Per nursing discretion.	Per nursing discretion.	Per nursing discretion; minimum one time in 24 hours.
Therapy/activities	Determined by level of responsibility.	Determined by level of responsibility; should always be accompanied by group.	Unit-based.
Room stripped	No.	Items (not sharp objects) contracted to be safe are available (e.g., radio, stuffed animals).	Yes.
Body check	Per nursing discretion.	Random.	Random, but done when staff index of suspicion is elevated.
Sharp objects	Used with supervision.	Used with direct one-to-one supervision.	No sharp objects. No smoking except on hourly schedule.
Meals	To be determined according to patient's nutritional status and intake (flow sheet).	Dependent on level of responsibility and nutritional status.	On unit, use flow sheet to document intake and nutritional status.
Unit supervision	Time alone in room to be monitored and structured as necessary.	When on unit, follows unit schedule, including kitchen supervision.	Follows unit schedule.
Charting	Flow sheet or progress note one time per shift with assessment of anger and isolation.	Flow sheet one time per shift with assessment of general thought processes, affect, anger, and isolation. Progress note once a day.	Flow sheet and progress note one time per shift with assessment of thought processes, anger, affect, isolation, and suicide potential.
Anger management	Journaling, relapse prevention plan, see nursing care plan.	Relapse prevention plan, encourage medications as needed, use of voluntary restraints.	Relapse prevention plan, encourage medications as needed, use of voluntary and involuntary restraints.
Maximum level of responsibility	Staff accompaniment. May be imposed and discontinued by nursing if required for no more than 8 hours.	Staff accompaniment.	Unit-restricted.

staff. An emphasis on safety should be a priority and should often be verbalized. Nursing staff members should carry gloves when working on a unit with self-mutilators, and the gloves should be put on before any physical intervention with a patient who has a wound.

Conclusion

Patient outcomes from the nursing interventions we have described should be specific, realistic, and short-term. An example of a realistic patient outcome is: The patient has a cognitive awareness of the pattern of behavior before and after self-mutilation. Another example: The patient is able to list the common here-and-now precipitants of the arousal state. It is even realistic, although usually uncomfortable, for nurses to write in a care plan that an intermediate outcome is to move from object insertion to scratching. We have not suggested a total cessation of self-mutilative behavior because it is usually unrealistic and would lead both the nurse and the patient to feel like failures.

The essence of fostering the personality development of a self-mutilating patient requires the patient to clearly realize that he or she is ultimately responsible for the behavior. At the same time, the nurse should attempt to bear the anxiety of not responding to self-mutilation with interventions similar to those exercised in response to a suicidal patient. Finally, the nurse and patient should work together in the positive direction of relapse prevention through development of insight and experiential skill-building.

References

Favazza, A.R. (1989). Why patients mutilate themselves. *Hospital and Community Psychiatry, 40,* 137-145.

Feldman, M.D. (1988). The challenge of self-mutilation: A review. *Comprehensive Psychiatry, 29,* 252-269.

Menninger, K.A. (1935). A psychoanalytic study of the significance of self-mutilations. *Psychoanalytic Quarterly, 4,* 408-466.

Pao, P. (1969). The syndrome of delicate self-cutting. *British Journal of Medical Psychology, 42,* 195-206.

Peplau, H.E. (1963). Interpersonal relations and the process of adaptation. *Nursing Science, 1,* 272-279.

Sebree, R., & Popkess-Vawter S. (1991). Self-injury concept formation: Nursing diagnosis development. *Perspectives in Psychiatric Care, 27*(2), 27-35.

van der Kolk, B.A. (1987). *Psychological trauma.* Washington, DC: American Psychiatric Press.

Walsh, B.W., & Rosen P.M. (1988). *Self-mutilation: Theory, research, and treatment.* New York: Guilford.

Winchel, R.M., & Stanley, M. (1991). Self-injurious behavior: A return of the behavior and biology of self-mutilation. *American Journal of Psychiatry, 148,* 306-317.

10. Multiple Personality Disorders: Treatment Coordination in a Partial Hospital Setting

Kay A. Kelly, MSW

Many patients with multiple personality disorder (MPD) can be effectively treated in a partial hospital setting. Partial hospital treatment teams and their patients develop and manage a safe transitional environment that contains the therapy and begins the process of independent functioning in the community. Not all patients with MPD can be treated in partial hospital settings. The author provides guidelines for appropriate placement of these patients.

The pathology of patients with multiple personality disorder (MPD) covers a wide range of severity. Thus a broad spectrum of resources and services are needed throughout the course of treatment. The mix might include options ranging from extended inpatient to extended outpatient psychotherapy. In this treatment continuum, the partial hospital service can provide maximum day, evening, and weekend structure and support while the patient explores traumatic issues as a psychotherapy outpatient. As financial constraints increase, partial hospital treatment with outpatient psychotherapy is becoming the long-term treatment of choice for many patients, including those with MPD. In this paper, I will provide guidelines for assessing whether a patient should be treated in the partial hospital setting, define the role of the treatment coordinator, and provide an outline for planning, developing, and monitoring treatment plans for such patients.

Partial hospital service settings provide a wide range of outpatient support for the patient with MPD. The patient's individual treatment program may include psychotherapy, hypnotherapy, and specific therapies as indicated—for example, alcohol, drug, and eating disorders counseling, biofeedback, and various educational programs. Other available resources encompass a full activity program, group psychotherapy, medication clinics, psychiatric consultations as needed, social work interventions, supported living environments, social interactions, vocational programs (including counseling, on-grounds work training, and supervision in community and volunteer employment), and treatment coordination. In the partial hospital program at The

This article is based on a presentation at a Menninger Continuing Education conference, "Dissociative States: Multiple Personality and Other Trauma-Related Disorders," held February 14-16, 1992, at Topeka, Kansas. Ms. Kelly is a staff social worker in the Partial Hospitalization Service at The Menninger Clinic.

Menninger Clinic, each treatment team meets 5 hours per week to plan and monitor treatment programs for 30-35 patients. Those with MPD are placed with other patients who have various diagnoses. The treatment team comprises a psychiatrist team leader, a nurse, social workers, and activity therapists.

Guidelines for partial hospital treatment

Patients learning to maintain themselves should be in the least restrictive environment possible. But the ability to form alliances, self-report, soothe oneself, and fulfill contracts is critical in a less structured environment; patients without these abilities are at increased risk of harm, and they should not be placed in a partial hospital setting. For many patients, however, these settings provide an optimal amount of structure through day programs, vocational training, and supervised living. The following guidelines can help staff members assess patients with MPD to determine whether they can be effectively treated in the partial hospital setting.

Suicidality and self-destructive behavior. What is the patient's history of suicide attempts? What is the status of current or previous eating disorders, alcohol or drug use or abuse, self-mutilation, excessive spending? How well does the patient verbalize impulses rather than act on them? What capacity does the patient have for self-reporting and discussing suicide and other self-destructive behaviors?

Motivation. Patient motivation is a basic factor in any successful treatment. How strong is the patient's commitment to work toward the resolution of separateness, avoidance, and dissociative defenses? Does the patient have the capacity to develop skills for cooperation and healthy coping? What are the patient's ego strengths and resources?

Dissociation/switching control. To what extent is the patient able to recognize his or her own resources and use them for personal benefit? What is the patient's level of awareness of situations and feelings that trigger switching or dissociative episodes? How well does the patient control day-to-day functioning (e.g., driving, following schedules)?

Ability to contract. How well can the patient develop and maintain an ongoing contract (i.e., an agreement to accomplish certain goals and refrain from destructive behavior in treatment)?

Abuser/victim paradigm. The patient's ability to form an alliance with outpatient treaters is essential given the decreased amount of structure in the partial hospital setting in comparison with inpatient treatment. To what degree does the patient re-create the abuser/victim pattern of relationships? Is the patient involved in an abusive relationship? If so, can he or she be treated? Can the abuser be brought into treatment so as to stop the abuse? Given that trust and treatment alliances are tentative at best, to what extent can the patient trust treaters?

Flashbacks, memories, and posttraumatic stress disorder symptoms. What are the patient's current symptoms? What coping skills does the patient use to deal with them? Is the patient aware that these symptoms are memories? Can he or she remain grounded in present reality?

Medication. What is the status of the patient's medication use? If the patient is heavily medicated or the medication regimen is not stabilized, a brief hospitalization may need to precede a partial hospital program (Braun, 1990).

Mapping. To what extent have the patient's various alters been identified? When did they come into existence? How many alters are there? Are they aware of each other? How collaborative are they in the treatment process?

Boundaries and containment. To what extent can the patient maintain boundaries between therapy and other treatment structures? Treaters recognize that boundary clarification is an ongoing issue, but containment of the exploratory work in the therapy process is a goal.

Family relationships and issues. What kinds of interference may be expected from the patient's family? What losses (e.g., financial resources, emotional support, potential or actual cut-offs from family members) may result from the patient's treatment? Legal issues that could affect patient and family should be clarified during the assessment process.

Indications for hospitalization

Maintaining the patient in the least restrictive environment can be achieved by balancing optimum functioning and safety. Several strategies might be implemented before resorting to hospitalization. If a patient with MPD resides in an apartment, could an evening or overnight stay be arranged at a supervised living structure? Is a weekend or evening program available? Are there programs that offer assistance at the patient's home—for example, clinical nurses who can provide adequate support to patients in crisis? Pacing the therapy and treatment can mitigate an impending crisis. Frequent meetings between the treatment coordinator and the psychotherapist help to balance therapy, control, and a safe environment for the patient. Such a balance supports the patient and solidifies the treatment approach, thus preventing polarization between treatment modalities.

If such strategies as contracts, medication adjustments, increased treatment structure, and slower paced therapy are ineffective, hospitalization may be indicated. For most patients, hospitalization should be brief and should focus on such specific problems as regrouping, depression, suicidal ideation, and the development of safety plans (Kluft, 1991; Turkus, 1991). More extended hospitalization may be needed to deal with regression, harm to self or others, and severe decompensation. Extreme decompensation, ongoing abuse, or intense pressure to hurt self or others may require even longer hospitalization (Kluft, 1991).

Role of the treatment coordinator

The treatment coordinator, who is responsible for overseeing all aspects of treatment, may be the partial hospital treatment team nurse, social worker, or activity therapist. The patient with MPD lives in a chaotic world, as manifested in an outward life-style of self-destructive thoughts, actions, other acting-out behavior, relationship difficulties, struggles for autonomy, and an inability to focus on goals. The treatment coordinator provides a reality base and introduces organizing mechanisms into this chaotic world. He or she works one-on-one with the patient to develop a safe environment that contains the therapy, provides treatment, and teaches the patient how to make decisions about self-care (Turkus, 1991). The patient is an active treatment participant responsible for behavior and recovery in the treatment process (Kluft, 1991; Turkus, 1991). Thus he or she should periodically be included in team meetings to review the treatment process and plan.

The treatment coordinator not only receives information from many treatment resources and the patient, but also informs other treaters about the patient's behavior, thoughts, and feelings. The treatment coordinator acts as the host treater responsible for working with the various parts of the treatment system for an integrated treatment approach. The clear metaphor of the integrated structure can provide a model for the patient with MPD who must work with the system of alters as a whole. In essence, these patients can learn to become their own treatment coordinator.

A consistent, integrated team approach involves dialogue and cooperation among team members. Such interaction, particularly in the area of problem solving, can model healthy behavior and provide supportive interpretation that leads to a higher level of integration by the patient (Turkus, 1991).

Treatment planning and monitoring

Because the patient with MPD is encouraged to take responsibility for all actions, healthy behavior, and appropriate treatment, the patient and treatment coordinator work together from the beginning of treatment to plan, develop, and monitor the program. The work focuses on identifying the problems, stating concrete and clear short-term and long-term goals, determining what resources to use, and estimating the time frames of treatment segments. Two or three problem areas are developed in a simple, focused way. Problem areas such as dissociation or other symptoms, relationship issues, and autonomy should be addressed.

Treatment plan considerations

The treatment plan must address a variety of factors based on the patient's individual circumstances. Dissociation is a major challenge that necessitates documentation of each patient's unique symptoms. Such symptoms may include confusion, anxiety, panic attacks, flashbacks, voices urging self-harm or suicide, rage, fear, psychotic-like thinking, self-criticism, cutting, overspending, burning, striking out, intrusiveness, phobias, food disturbances, or stealing. Working with patients to choose two or three goals for addressing the problem of dissociation can begin to help them gain mastery over their complex and complicated internal world.

Patient safety is also a concern. In a partial hospital setting, the patient's ability to work with the treatment coordinator to assess lethality is essential. Patients are expected to work toward keeping their body safe. They must report self-critical and destructive thoughts and voices and suicidal ideation or plans to the treatment coordinator. These patients, however, are crisis-prone; alters may be struggling with each other (Kluft, 1991). The internal chaos may lead to traumatic reenactment of external chaos and confusion with the environment (Turkus, 1991).

Flashbacks may occur in the partial hospital setting. Identification of flashback triggers and the establishment of a safe place (either physically or emotionally) can help patients gain control over past traumas. Patients who can talk about the memory as a past event and state the current reality are more likely to remain grounded in the present.

Patient contracts

Because MPD is associated with fragmentation and discontinuity, its treatment requires clear, straightforward written and verbal communi-

119

cation. One useful form of communication is a contract in which the patient agrees to: (1) report self-destructive feelings, thoughts, actions, and plans; (2) use self-soothing strategies; (3) select safe places and people; (4) choose healthy interactions; (5) use daytime structure appropriately; (6) leave daily notes for treatment coordinators concerning current level of functioning; (7) schedule telephone check-ins; (8) call the treatment coordinator prior to self-destructive or suicidal acts or for emergency hospitalizations; and (9) drive safely.

Contract outlines that include the patient's suggestions tend to be more comprehensive than treaters might develop by themselves. One patient's contract included the following guidelines for the use of his car:

(1) naming the adult alters who would and could drive; (2) obeying traffic rules; (3) stating a curfew time; (4) outlining the procedures for what to do if an alter becomes suicidal while driving (pull over and gain control, discontinue driving until impulses are manageable, take a cab, walk, turn in keys to treatment staff until control is regained); (5) outlining a daily driving schedule so treaters know the patient's whereabouts; and (6) driving only to and from activities, work, and volunteer activities.

One patient in a supervised living program designed the following plan for management of dissociative episodes:

Mild dissociative states that include feeling restless, edgy, withdrawn, and unable to concentrate may be alleviated by distractions such as talking to others, relaxing with music, spending time alone, or focusing on a project or idea. However, when dissociative states intensify, focusing becomes more difficult and agitation increases. At such times, it is more helpful to be with other people, perhaps walking with a friend or talking through issues with staff. It is hard to ask for help, but when the intrusive, destructive thoughts begin, I need companionship. Relaxation in a rocking chair, medication as needed, relaxing tapes, and sleep may help, but if nothing works, I will call my treatment coordinator to assess the need for hospitalization.

For the patient who is unsure about what procedure to follow, the written plan facilitates access to the support of the treatment staff and treatment coordinator. Copies of the narrative should be distributed to the treatment team, the patient, supervised living staff, psychotherapists, and any other person involved in the patient's treatment. Limits in supervised living programs can be set up in contract form. The patient should design the contract with supervision by the living staff and the treatment coordinator. The contract should include halfway house expectations, appropriate times to discuss treatment issues with halfway house staff members, specified times to call the treatment coordinator or other treaters, consequences for violent outbursts (e.g., automatic rehospitalization), appropriate television programs or movies (none of an upsetting nature), and a time frame for reviewing the contract (e.g., after 2-3 weeks), at which time revisions may be made. Contracts are signed and dated by all parties.

Boundaries

MPD is a disorder of broken boundaries. The goals of the treatment plan should include setting firm limits and boundaries to contain maladaptive and self-defeating behavior; strengthening the patient's capacity to delay, anticipate, and tolerate anxiety; and helping the patient achieve a strong sense of autonomy.

Treatment coordinators often find it difficult to set firm limits on after-hour telephone calls, which should be limited to emergencies. The treatment coordinator is usually the first-contact treater for such a call. Although the treatment coordinator should be accessible to the patient, the process must be structured so that accessibility remains respectful, nonintrusive, and nonabusive. The treatment coordinator must convey the message that he or she is not there solely to support one individual patient. Kluft (1990) has recommended that calls should be in the range of 3-7 minutes.

Patients with MPD should be encouraged to develop self-soothing tools. Such techniques, used prior to contacting the treatment coordinator, may include reading (not violent or abusive material), deep-breathing exercises, listening to relaxation tapes, exercising, guided imagery, crying, internal dialogue with alters for problem solving and decision making, journaling, music, walking, inner self-helpers, medications as needed, singing, prayer, hot baths, hot tea, planning meetings, connecting with supportive friends, and buying something special for self or others.

Treaters must set boundaries and protect themselves when working with these difficult patients. For example, one patient with multiple personality disorder called treaters nightly, sometimes talking for as long as an hour. Such a practice is unrealistic for the treatment team and may cause unnecessary regression in the patient. Firm limit-setting eventually reduced the patient's after-hour phone calls to one short, supportive, reality-focused call per week at a mutually convenient time. On the other hand, some patients with MPD fail to make after-hour calls when they should. Supportive care for these patients includes developing a strategy to help them determine when a call is necessary.

Some patients are keenly aware of the boundaries and can keep therapy and treatment separate from work, social situations, volunteer jobs, and living programs.

Treatment strategies

Journaling can help MPD patients contain affect. A journal is a readily available and self-paced healing tool that provides object constancy and catharsis; it is also a witness to the shifts and changes in the patient's world. Use of a journal can teach patients to reflect rather than react. Journals are a source of pride and self-esteem, and can provide clarity to the patient who works and reworks treatment issues.

Relationships

The interpersonal relationships of MPD patients often reflect their past broken-down family boundaries. Symptoms are unique to each patient and may include a low level of trust, conflictual relationships, fears of separation and independence, inability to express needs, distortions, strained parental relationships, withdrawal, isolation, and difficulties sharing feelings.

The treatment coordinator works closely with the team social worker to understand how the patient's family dynamics interplay within the team and peer relationships. The social worker assigned to the family of origin or current family addresses relationship issues through whatever level of contact can be made with the patient and family members. Through these contacts, the social worker seeks historical family data that might improve understanding of the patient's dysfunctional status. Useful information might include how family members have traditionally responded to authority, and how they have dealt with such issues as separation and individuation, traumatic events, and parental stress. The social worker can also help family members understand the nature of the patient's illness.

If social skills training is not provided in the activity program, the treatment coordinator may need to offer such training in one-on-one sessions. This training can help the patient learn how to: listen and respond, ask for help, become assertive, negotiate, say no, apologize, resolve conflicts, solve problems, set goals, and engage in appropriate conversations. The patient's sense of withdrawal and isolation is addressed by encouraging increased socialization, development of friendships, leisure time activities, and weekend plans. Patients with MPD can increase their connectedness with others by attending and participating in the activity program. Activities such as weekend planning, recreational skills, men's and women's groups, hiking, arts and art therapy, current events, budgeting, basic cooking, bibliotherapy, and soap opera therapy* improve connectedness with others and the community. Partial hospital settings can help the patient take the necessary transitional steps toward integration into the community.

Autonomy

In the partial hospital setting, the patient with MPD becomes increasingly responsible for a personal daily routine. Because time misuse and avoidance are symptoms of the disorder, time management, attendance, and participation in daily activity structures and therapies become necessary goals. Tools such as lists, alarm watches, medication boxes, organizers, Post-it pads, journals, and frequent calendar checking can help the patient deal with day-to-day responsibilities (Turkus, 1991).

Patients are expected to attend the outlined daily structure. If unable to attend, they are also expected to assume the responsibility of informing the activity or group leader. Problems with attendance or participation are brought first to the patient and then to the treatment coordinator. The activity therapist may work with the treatment coordinator and patient in an effort to resolve problems. On occasion, the treatment coordinator may need to approve all appointments if they are scheduled at the same time as the activities. Thus there is no confusion about a patient's whereabouts at any given time. As the patient begins to master daily functioning in a day hospital setting, vocational counseling and future plans assume a prominent role in treatment. Vocational planning includes occupational assessments, vocational rehabilitation referrals, testing, job seeking skills, on-grounds vocational training, and volunteer or paid employment in the community. The vocational counselor is the link between the patient, the treatment coordinator, and the supervisor in a volunteer or work setting.

Often the patient with MPD has not lived independently in a successful manner. Both patient and family members may need help with such matters as credit card management, budgeting, social security issues, trust funds, and insurance. The treatment coordinator can help the patient find appropriate resources. The patient's preparation for transition from structured living and partial hospital programs can be carried out over an extended period. Anticipation and evaluation of the patient's fears, dissociative episodes, self-destructive behavior (e.g.,

---

*Soap opera therapy, which has been in use for a number of years (Falk-Kessler & Froschauer, 1978; Kilguss, 1974, 1977), combines group therapy with social interactive experience through use of a one-hour television series to stimulate discussion of social, family, and relationship issues. It was introduced to the Menninger Partial Hospitalization Service by Marianne Hund, MS, ATR.

eating disorders, overspending, suicidal thoughts), and available coping mechanisms will ease transitions and help the patient maintain an optimal level of functioning.

Consultations can be extremely helpful to treaters. Formal yearly consultations by in-house staff are recommended. Additional consultations may be needed for specific treatment areas (e.g., alcohol and drug abuse, eating disorders). Consultations should be sought when unusual or special treatment is given to the patient (Kluft, 1990). When a treatment team becomes polarized regarding the treatment of a particular patient, a consultation can help diffuse the intensity that these patients can generate among their treaters.

References

Adams, M.A. (1989). Internal self helpers of persons with multiple personality disorder. *Dissociation, 2*(3), 138-143.

Braun, B. (1990, November). *Treatment planning and the steps of treatment*. Paper presented at the Seventh International Conference on Multiple Personality/Dissociative States, Chicago.

Falk-Kessler, J., & Froschauer, K.H. (1978). The soap opera: A dynamic group approach for psychiatric patients. *American Journal of Occupational Therapy, 32,* 317-319.

Kilguss, A.F. (1974). Using soap operas as a therapeutic tool. *Social Casework, 55,* 525-530.

Kilguss, A.F. (1977). Therapeutic use of a soap opera discussion group with psychiatric in-patients. *Clinical Social Work Journal, 5,* 58-65.

Kluft, R.P. (1990, November). *Pragmatics and crisis intervention*. Paper presented at the Seventh International Conference on Multiple Personality/Dissociative States, Chicago.

Kluft, R.P. (1991). Multiple personality disorder. In A. Tasman & S.M. Goldfinger (Eds.), *American Psychiatric Press review of psychiatry* (Vol. 10, pp. 161-188). Washington, DC: American Psychiatric Press.

Turkus, J.A. (1991). Psychotherapy and case management for multiple personality disorders: Synthesis for continuity of care. *Psychiatric Clinics of North America, 14,* 649-660.

Index